ANOTHER VIRGIN SOLDIER

Wartime initiations of a "Cotswold Boy" conscript

JIM LAZENBY

To Peter & Wendy
Best Wishes & Happy 2008

Jim Lazenby

First Published in 2007

Published by Jim Lazenby 2007

© Jim Lazenby

ISBN 978-0-9555876-9-6

Acknowledgements

Mr Robin J. Brookes who has so generously allowed me to include "Whatever material I wish" from his own excellent book "Oxfordshire Airfields in the Second World War", one of his series which covers much of the British Isles.

Barry Cooper, secretary to the Fairford Classic Car Club for photographs of cars and aeroplanes.

Bill King, member of the Military Vehicle Trust. Avid researcher into many aspects of wartme relics and still identifiable sites, for facts and photographs.

Particular praise for the same dedicated team who made my first book a reality:

Libby Davies who kick-started me again and transcribed my long-hand scrawl into computer print.

Mary Tudge, who accomplished the preparation needed for the book lay-out, despite her many other commitments.

David Shayler for again managing to produce the polished and finished book regardless of the pressures of his thriving printing business.

Also the many readers of my first book who seem to have waited, with sometimes ill-concealed impatience, but have also spurred me on. I imagine some surprises may now await them!

INTRODUCTION

Ever since I read Leslie Thomas's acclaimed book The Virgin Soldier and saw the subsequent film I have nurtured the notion that I should commit my experiences of World War 2 and its impact on this bit of England, to paper.

Most such books are written by, or about, wartime heroes. That the majority of our Servicemen, conscripted to serve their country, have left their own stories untold, seems a serious oversight. To have been engaged in frontline action was not the only criterion for having a tale to tell. As will become obvious, many of the questionable and surprising events I so vividly recall could not have been acknowledged, or related, until these many years have elapsed.

Or shall I still be subjected to visits from government officials and calls from enraged citizens representing our recently passed laws of political correctness and racial equality for describing the Black Market with its inevitable corruption, as well as the notion of white supremacy which was endemic, particularly in the U.S. forces. I hope not, as I earnestly believe that the attitudes which then prevailed should be faithfully and honestly recorded, so that our advances in the understanding and appreciation of our fellow men may be more fully realised.

I am privileged to recommended another book
"A Burford Boy" Written by his daughter Sue Shayler, it details the truly intriguing life of Bob Pearman, late of "Paine and Pearman" the erstwhile "Cotswold Gateway Garage" at the top of Burford.

His story from boyhood to R.A.F. Pilot Officer relating his many experiences as a wartime bomber pilot who completed a full "tour" of operational flights and his extraordinary survivals, is fascinating and compulsory reading.

CHAPTER ONE

Enough of School!

"How long do you think it will last this time?"

"Not long enough to worry us."

"My dad was in the last one and we all hope that he won't get called up this time."

"It'll be over in no time."

"That's what they said last time and it went on for over four years. My Uncle Harry was killed, in France."

"So was my Uncle Bob, but he was sunk at sea."

"Be nice if they bombed the school one night and old Bassett (Headmaster) was in there."

Such was the eager conversation on Pulham's school bus the first day of the autumn term in September 1939.

War with Germany had just been announced by Neville Chamberlain. Yes, the same Prime Minister who, a year before, had negotiated such an understanding with Adolf Hitler of Germany, that to the relief of most, he flew home brandishing a weighty document and declaring, "Peace in our time". Though in most eyes, people, and indeed historians, have judged him for perceived weakness, this treaty bought valuable time. It was employed in reviewing the state of our country's readiness, should another threat arise in the future and it was found seriously lacking. The numbers, the size and the general capacity of its Air Force were rapidly re-drawn. This inevitably began an ever-increasing change to the locality, its villages and inhabitants.

I was now thirteen years old. My birthday had been in June. Two years before I had sailed through the entrance exam for Northleach Grammar School. Sailed is an apt description. There had been several subjects to choose from when writing an essay for the English paper. Mr. Gibbs, Headmaster of Great Barrington School, later expressed his consternation when I had chosen to write about ships. But all was well. By chance I had recently read a book on their development, through dugouts, coracles, sailing ships to ocean liners. The exam results were so good that after a further test held at Rendcomb College, I was offered a place there. At that time they supplied two full scholarships and two half fees for their catchment area. I won a half fee place; Mother was quite thrilled. Then to my relief, Father, who could easily have managed to, declined to put up the money. To become a dayboy at Northleach was so much more desirable than to be banished off to board at Rendcomb.

The school bus, one of several contracted from Pulham's of Bourton to transport the boys and girls was an old Reo. It was the oldest in the fleet, being the only charabanc, with a collapsible roof and artillery-spoked wheels. It served the Bourton, Clapton and Sherborne area. It came only as far as the east end of Sherborne and turned back there. This meant that the unfortunate scholars from the Barringtons had to cycle some three miles each way to catch it. The eleven year-olds, going on fifteen, braved this all year round test of weather, hills and dales. At the time they didn't appreciate just how good it must be for their physical, even mental welfare in those pre- and adolescent years.

Mr Tremaine, at the first farm, graciously allowed the pupils to leave their bicycles in a stone barn opposite the back door of his farmhouse. My companions at that time were Philip Hands and Maurice Herbert, both bigger, older and in higher school classes. Boys will be boys, and after parking their bikes some horseplay took over. So it was with some fear that I would hear Maurice say, "Come on you deserve a slap on the back for that." I'd then have my arms pinned while my collar was eased away from my neck and several lumpy bits of coke were pushed down. A hearty slap on the back and a cheery "Well done, Jim", caused a "coke rash", more painful than a gravel rash.

After stopping to pick up Les Hayward, Harry Taylor, Henry Shepherd and others, the old bus groaned its way up to the A40 and thence to Northleach having met the Cheltenham–Oxford 171 service bus. Also the Black and White coach making its regular journey from Cheltenham to London. The Black and White coaches were the "crème de la crème" and monopolised the bus routes, which radiated all over the country, from its busy terminus in Cheltenham. They eventually formed an important part of the future National Express Company.

The then modern Westwoods, built in the 20's to succeed the original grammar school in the middle of the town but now bulldozed to allow the inevitable rash of housing development, stood proudly above and overlooking extensive playing fields.

After assembly and a welcome back to the last year's pupils and the new intake, the headmaster Mr W. P. Bassett – nicknamed "Waste Paper Basket" – dismissed them all to their new classrooms. Here I was amazed to find that the huge windows, which took up most of the south walls, already sported a criss-cross of black tape to help prevent them from blowing in should a bomb explode nearby. Big blackout curtains soon appeared for dark winter evenings.

School continued much as before. The same pals were there to discuss the events of their long summer vacation.

Don Pritchard, the Chedworth railway station-master's son; Tony Bray, who would later join the Vestey's Blue Funnel Shipping line and would eventually become harbourmaster of the port of Buenos Aires; Gerald Gaden, farmers son; and many others.

But this is not "Tom Brown's Schooldays" and suffice it to say that after gaining an impressive School Certificate I left. Enough of Westwoods.

CHAPTER TWO

The R.A.F. and Early Wartime

Great Barrington, or rather the people of the village and others around, soon sensed a big change. A surge in the activities at Little Rissington aerodrome made the first impact. It was No. 6 SFTS (Service Flying Training School) and quite quickly opened the south section to form No.8 M.U. (Maintenance Unit). 6 SFTS had become operational in August 1938 when it moved from Nether Avon with its Harts and Audaxes, a few Furies and soon afterwards a few Avro Ansons.

Number 8 M.U. handled Spitfires and Wellingtons. On September 3rd 1939 there were well over two hundred aircraft stored there.

6 SFTS had an elementary course, flying the smaller planes and an advanced squadron of American built Harvards with Ansons and Oxfords from which the pilots went for operational training.

The first winter was a hard one, snow causing cessation of flying and it was acutely necessary to make plans to cover those periods. Rissington now had over four hundred aircraft and so satellite facilities were established. Windrush R.L.G. (Relief Landing Ground) was prepared and ready for use in July 1940. On July 29th a German aircraft released bombs meant for Rissington. They landed nearly three miles away but caused a decision to be taken that night flying instruction should take place at Windrush and complete blackout observed at the vulnerable Rissington establishment. Other 'dromes mushroomed at Northleach, Bibury, Chedworth, Chipping Norton, Bradwell Grove and Hook's landing ground at Southrop. The one at Akeman Street north of Witney later became a day–night flying instruction airstrip. Here, landing lights along the runway were kept burning all day. The pupils in their aircraft were made to pull a smoky glass visor over their eyes, which gave the impression of a night landing approach.

Most, like Windrush, were grass areas with steel mesh laid and pegged down to

Avro Anson

Hawker Hart

North American Harvard

form the runways and a perimeter track.

Windrush became a self-contained unit. Flight control tower, blister hangers and hutments to accommodate a ground crew capable of administering the needs of two flights, mainly composed of Oxfords but with a few Ansons. Also a N.A.A.F.I. (Navy, Army & Airforce Institute), a sergeants' mess and adequate underground bomb shelters.

Much of this, ironically, surrounding the old but still very recognisable Windrush Camp, an Iron Age encampment still surrounded by earthwork ramparts. Both situated on that high plateau but representing two very different styles of defence.

Soon all able-bodied men of eighteen years and over became liable for conscription into one or other of the armed forces. There was also the establishment of the L.D.V's (Local Defence Volunteers). Those in this area were usually made up of veterans from World War One, farmers, young men not yet "called up" and the local squires. No uniform and little armament other than their own shotguns was available. The various ranks were handed out. Farmers and gentry became the officers and the veterans were appointed as N.C.O's. Thus, in Barrington, Farmer Jack Hendey became a Lieutenant and Harry Cambray the sergeant. Later, when uniforms arrived and America supplied a number of their stock of old First World War rifles, the name Home Guard was adopted from one of Churchill's rallying calls.

Sadly, today, most people's perception of the Home Guard has been gleaned from the amusing sequences as retold in the television programme "Dad's Army". Certainly all members can recall strange and funny situations but to be out there during bitter winter weather, wondering whether the German paratroops, as strongly predicted, would be landing in the area, was no picnic.

The huge influx of R.A.F. personnel to Windrush and Rissington aerodromes brought many motorcars. The aspiring pilots, so many of them from families of wealth and status, found that the introduction of strict petrol rationing made it impossible for them to use their own transport. This created a surplus of magnificent vehicles, now redundant, so that Green Label Bentleys and the like were disposed of for a paltry £50 or so. Those that survived are now amongst the most valuable and cherished cars of all time.

An S.S. One

Charles Silvertop, a seriously wealthy young farmer of Upton Downs Farm, created storage and filled some of his barns with Rolls-Royces, Bentleys and other expensive vehicles ferried down from London. At one time he had his own light aircraft and used a landing strip by his house. He could pull a few strings and lived a very fast life. One reported story concerned a London lass with whom he'd spent a night in a grand hotel room. She made certain allegations about him, hoping for recompense, but in a London court he was able to convince the jury that, though having spent the night in the ladies bed, nothing improper had happened.

"The bedroom décor was not conducive to such actions." He hadn't liked the wallpaper!

Austin 10

The young man died at only thirty-nine years old, probably having drunk himself to death. On clearing out the property "wagon loads" of empty gin bottles had to be moved.

My father had bought a memorable car from an R.A.F. officer before the war. It was an SSOne, a very impressive sporting saloon, precursor to the S.S. Jaguar. He was extremely proud of it and took the family on a very rare outing to the Hendon Air Display. It was 1937 and the aeroplane that caught my eye was the Gloster Gladiator. Several carried out mock attacks on a dummy fortress. The Gladiator was later immortalised as the only air defence for Malta during that island's worst period. The three left to engage the enemy were fondly known as Faith, Hope and Charity.

This London foray disclosed a huge variation in petrol prices. At Barrington it sold at one shilling and three-halfpence a gallon, whereas R.O.P. petrol was on sale for ten pence halfpenny a gallon. Naturally it was said to be inferior, or was it? R.O.P. stood for Russian Oil Products, but was soon dubbed "Russian 'oss piss".

Citroen "Twenty" floating power

Sadly, the SSOne was sold to another R.A.F. officer who was killed when he crashed it through the parapet of a railway bridge and it fell onto the lines below.

My father with his garage, petrol forecourt, motor repair business and taxi service was overwhelmed. With little personal transport of their own the R.A.F. boys had to rely on buses and taxis to take them to catch trains at local railways stations. This need generated a great deal of work for the local taxis. Kingham Junction, as indeed it then was, at the end of the line from Cheltenham, after its trip through Andoversford, Bourton-on-the-Water,

Standard "Flying Twelve"

Stow-on-the-Wold and other "halts", was the nearest station for Rissington 'drome. With only three cars, an Austin 10, a Standard Flying Twelve and a Ford V8, it became increasingly difficult for my father to satisfy the demand.

Kingham Station Garage sat on a goldmine. The owner, Mr Wells, and his sons were always within hail. They weren't happy when other taxis, having brought passengers down, waited on the next train's arrival to get a return fare. It could be a hazardous journey in bad weather. There are thirteen near right-angle bends on the short drive from the Stow road to the station!

To add to my father's problems his right hand man, Walter Preston, was directed to work on tank production at Abingdon. Also his apprentice Tony Pether, a son of the Burford builder, soon volunteered for aircrew. He was shot down and killed. A grievous loss.

The vacuum in the business had to be filled somehow. This meant that I had to help out during my leisure hours and Fred Russell, a big beefy farm worker, exempt from military service (as were many more whose job it was to grow ever more produce) also assisted.

Soon, War Agricultural advisors were appointed. It was their function to bring every acre of available land into food production. Their powers were considerable. Mr Jack Wakefield, farmer of Signet Hill, was one. Many tracts of hitherto scrub land, often very poor and covered with gorse, were put to the plough. The big area known as Westwell Gorse was typical.

Our first experience of overseas troops arriving was early in 1940. In the darkness of the black out, from home, several big fires were seen near the location of the garage on the A40 road, a mile away. I, with my father, worried that the garage was burning down, drove there quickly to investigate. We were shocked to find a convoy of Canadian troops camped there for the night. They were in their Canadian Ram tanks and had driven, off-road straight through the big hedge into the adjacent field leaving several big gaps. The flames were from raging camp fires, flamed by generous application of petrol.

Next day they had gone, but besides destroying the hedge it was found that their tanks seemed to have systematically torn most of the "cats eyes" out of the centre of the road.

Such "vandalism" had never been seen before but was to herald many other such "antics" over the years to come.

By now Windrush aerodrome was opening up. The threat of invasion by air was evidenced by the siting of a whole mixture of derelict vehicles around the perimeter. They were to serve as obstacles and would be towed onto the airfield to prevent the enemy from landing! Not a very inspired idea, time could hardly have allowed it. Also, as the war years advanced and spare parts and tyres became impossible for many to obtain, the old wrecks were robbed of anything remotely useful, including wheels and tyres, leaving them quite immobile.

Petroleum was now supplied under the common name of "Pool Petrol". The familiar lighted globes on the top of the pumps remained in their varied shapes, advertising Shell, BP, National Benzole, Cleveland Discol, etc. Petrol rationing became ever more stringent and was firmly applied. Petrol coupons of varied denominations were issued. They were either black "basic" allowances or red ones issued to the most essential users. In this district the red ones applied more to the farming community. Farm tractors all ran on T.V.O. – tractor vaporising oil – except for petrol for starting and warming them up, before switching over to the T.V.O., which was very similar to paraffin. Service vehicles ran on petrol, which was dyed red. If it was used illegally, it was easily detected and stained the carburettor. Aviation fuel, 100 octane instead of the pool at 71 octane was dyed green and would quickly burn the valves out on a car engine.

Several R.A.F. officers cars were kept "off camp" at the Barrington Filling Station. They had to be.

It was soon discovered that a balanced mixture of household paraffin – on which there was no restriction – aviation fuel and some pool petrol could be mixed for car use. Too much paraffin always produced smoke and a sweet smell when used and was a dead giveaway. There was an art in achieving the optimum quantities.

About this time huge petrol tankers began to call at the garage. They didn't hang around. The drivers would claim that on off-loading at the aerodrome their tanks had failed to discharge the last fifty gallons or so because of uneven ground! There was then a very convenient arrangement with my father to take this "residue". Everyone a winner. The driver, the garage and the customers.

Another source of copious supply developed later on when huge Massey-Harris 21 combine-harvesters were imported from America. These and the later 726 model ran solely on petrol. The farmers with them received a very generous allowance of petrol coupons. They "banked" them at the garage and drew fuel on them until their next allocation.

The garage simply kept all coupons, basic, essential and farm in a tin box. When a load of say five hundred gallons was delivered the tanker driver had to receive the equivalent number in a sealed envelope. Not surprisingly there was always an excess, making it possible to supply the local customers with extra fuel.

One day I noticed that one pump was sporting an army gaiter buckled around the "sight glass". This contraption, common to all pumps, allowed the customer to watch the fuel spin a disc as it was delivered into his tank.

"What's that for Dad?" I asked.

"Ah, don't you worry about it" was the reply.

It transpired that an illegal delivery, had, without warning, dropped a quantity of "red" fuel in, thereby discolouring all that in the underground tank. Father got away with it but not without a real scare.

At regular intervals the Customs "Weights and Measures" inspector would make a visit. He would fill his measures to make sure the pumps were dispensing accurately. To my father's horror he came during this crisis. Having recognised him the following conversation ensued.

"Hello, how are you? Didn't expect you yet."

"Well, thought it's time I came."

"Lovely day, isn't it?" – Not bad for a man deep in shock!

"Yes, I'm just going into the inn to check their measures."

The old man nearly collapsed with relief.

The same distinction was made between "private" car owners and "essential" citizens in the supply of spare parts. Nothing for the private owner, but after much form filling, a trickle of the most vulnerable parts, clutches, tyres, axle shafts, bearings and so on, could be obtained for the "essential" man.

Again, this supply seemed to be augmented by visits from the store managers of the various suppliers, Ford, Austin dealers, etc. They enjoyed a drive out from Oxford or Cheltenham knowing full well they'd be able to have their petrol tanks filled and money in their wallets for the "under the counter" spare parts they brought with them.

I by this time, had been pressured into getting home from school, having a quick tea and cycling up to help father in the garage, and man the petrol pumps. This also included the weekend. All this to the dismay of my mother who even then could foresee the eventual curtailing and disruption of my academic potential. But this was one of the penalties of wartime necessity. This arrangement suffered a very temporary setback after one incident.

We three schoolboys, bent on getting home from Sherborne, raced each other at some speed. Our cycles all had what was commonly called "drop handlebars". These meant that, with head down to reach them, forward vision was only achieved by looking up briefly. I, as the youngest tried really hard to keep up. Then one day, riding through Windrush and following the curb I forgot that a vehicle could be parked there. My speed came to an abrupt halt when I encountered the rear of Fosters "shop on wheels". This mobile shop sold mainly kitchenware and ironmongery. My head struck the centre of a tin bath hanging on the rear, smiting a large dent in it. How I didn't break my neck no one knows. After some confusion, helped by the driver who was keen to know who would pay for his bath, I managed to re-mount again and ride home. It soon became obvious that the cycle had suffered too. My progress was made more uncomfortable because it was accompanied by a regular bounce at every turn of the wheels. To everyone's surprise the front wheel was fine but the back one now had a few inches of flattened rim. My weight had descended on it in a big way.

Amazingly enough I was only aware of a stiff neck. Years afterwards it was found that my skull had suffered several fractures!

The ever-helpful Mr Harry Barnes, the estate foreman, who in his spare time repaired bicycles in his shed at home, came to the rescue. He knocked the tin bath back into shape for its next ride on the mobile shop and repaired the bike wheel.

As the rigors of wartime existence bit ever harder, so did cars become more dangerous and less reliable. Tyres were deemed serviceable until the canvas, that corded base on to which the rubber was moulded, started to wear through. Stacks of previously discarded tyres were combed through, time and again. When all else failed an old, say, 19-inch tyre would be forced over the existing 18 inch one. When inflated it would last a short while. I even remember one chap with a little Austin 7, who, unable even to purchase a tube, stuffed his tyre with hay.

My father was adjudged to be on essential work and was excused from joining the Home Guard.

Sorties by lone German bombers now began. Small brick buildings surmounted by decoy beacons were built. Manned by R.A.F. personnel their purpose was to confuse the enemy. The one for R.A.F. Windrush was situated on the right of Leys Road just to the north of the farm house. That for Rissington was on the left, some 200 yards south of the turn to Great Rissington when approached from Barrington. The chaps attending them became sitting ducks. A few bombs were dropped, some blasting a clump of trees on the right hand side about a mile north of Great Barrington.

German bombers were easily identified at night by their engine sound, a distinctive "vrmm-vrmm". The night of the Coventry bombing was unreal. The armada of planes passed overhead making this dreaded noise and many returned by the same route.

The head gamekeeper on the Barrington estate was Alf Jennings. His son Tom was my best friend. We two walked the fields and hedgerows, helping to frustrate poachers with their traps and snares. One memorable morning we were walking a hedge, just one field removed from the eastern boundary of Windrush 'drome. Across here runs the ancient "Saltway", one of the packhorse trails, which brought the important salt to so many areas. Then suddenly we were confronted by a strange sight. Four bombs destined for the aerodrome, only a few hundred yards away, were standing, close to each other, with their noses in the soft ground. The sun gleamed on their shining cases and the erect tail fins. How stupid can fourteen-year-old boys be? Far from running for dear life, we condemned them as duds and inspected each one. They varied in size. The smallest was shaken to try to lift it out. What a trophy to carry home!

We decided against it and walked away unscathed. No one knew of this discovery until my father reported it. The R.A.F. Regiment guards were posted to watch over them from a very safe distance until a bomb disposal squad dealt with them.

The night of August 18th 1940 brought more excitement; I was awakened by several loud explosions. Soon after there came a tapping at my bedroom window which was the only one overlooking the road. Half asleep I opened it. Some members of the Home Guard were gathered near the war memorial and a familiar voice was heard. "Go and get your father up and tell him to bring his gun."

This was an ancient trigger-action twelve-bore.

"The German paratroops have landed and we've got to stop them."

Experiencing a mounting excitement I sped along the landing and performed the unthinkable sin of knocking loudly on my parents bedroom door.

"What do you want?"

"Dad, the Germans have landed and the Home Guard want you to take your gun and help them."

A wait, while the news was digested, a muffled conversation, a very long pause and, "Tell them I'm not going and that's that."

Unable to believe my ears I asked for confirmation. A determined voice repeated, "I'm not coming." Oh, the innocent naivety of the patriotic boy. What sort of a coward was my father? In retrospect, long before I reached his age, at that time, I found myself in absolute sympathy with his reaction. Especially so when it was found that no paratroopers had landed and that he would have spent a cold, muddy and quite useless night.

Bruce Hancock

The explosions had been bombs at Windrush airfield. A Heinkel, piloted by thirty year old Alfod Dreker who had flown his plane to bomb Brize Norton, seems to have been distracted to Windrush, made a bomb run at five hundred feet and dropped a stick of eleven-bombs, one of which exploded the next day. He turned to make a second attack. It was then the crew noticed a R.A.F. training aircraft ahead of them and the front gunner opened up with his machine gun. The aircraft was an Anson with twenty-six year old Sergeant Bruce Hancock at the controls. He switched off his navigation lights but was hit in the shoulder. He was in a hopeless situation. Reacting bravely he pulled his aircraft up into the path of the Heinkel. The nose smashed into its wing with great force. Whether this manoeuvre was deliberate or accidental will never be known.

Both aircraft crashed into adjoining fields. The remaining bombs exploded. No one escaped. The time was 10:45pm.

Fred Ind and Jack Parrott from Aldsworth were first on the scene. Soon, others arrived. Fred who'd been directing them into the field was grabbed by an R.A.F. sergeant, bundled into a truck and carted off to Little Rissington. Poor Fred had been suspected of being an enemy agent. All those of us that knew him would know that a less probable suspect it would be hard to imagine.

A memorial to Sergeant Hancock was quite recently let into the outside wall of Windrush churchyard to record this sacrifice.

All of this R.A.F. activity caused a familiarity with the service life and prompted many local lads to join the Burford branch of the Air Training Corps 1315 Squadron. I became a very enthusiastic member, along with Tom Jennings, Jack Stocks, Phillip Hands and others. We were very smart in our R.A.F. blue uniforms.

Airspeed Oxford

A new world opened up. Classes were held in the old Burford Grammar School buildings. Captain Dodd, ex-army, was Flying Officer in charge. Quite sophisticated courses were run on Navigation, Morse code,

Heinkel He 111, used on attacks on Oxfordshire airfields

School days   *New Soldier*

It is with a view to preparing myself for war-time service with either the Royal Air Force or the Fleet Air Arm or the Royal Navy (*cross out what does not apply*) that I am joining the Air Training Corps.

I hereby solemnly promise on my honour to serve this Unit loyally, and to be faithful to my obligations as a member of the Air Training Corps.

I further promise to be a good Citizen, honouring my King, my Country and its Flag.

(*Signature.*)

PARENT OR GUARDIAN'S CONSENT :

I consent to my son (or ward) joining the

AIR TRAINING CORPS

Date .... Signed ....

(5370) Wt. 38924—2817 50,0'0 1/41 T.S. 700
(0681· 5370) Wt. 45146—3365 100M 3/41 T.S. 709

Commitment to A.T.C. and to honour King and country

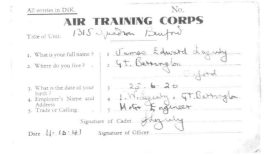

All entries in INK.   No.
AIR TRAINING CORPS
Title of Unit. 1315 Squadron Burford

1. What is your full name ?   1 James Edward Lagenby
2. Where do you live ?   .   2 Gt. Barrington
                                  Oxford
3. What is the date of your   3 25. 6. 20
   birth ?
4. Employer's Name and   4 I. N. Lagenby. Gt. Barrington.
   Address
5. Trade or Calling.   .   5 Motor Engineer

          Signature of Cadet Lagenby
Date ..(. (o . 4.)   Signature of Officer ....

which included receiving as well as sending messages – physical training in the gym and parade ground skills. We were all there by choice and applied ourselves fully.

Examinations were held for promotions. They were a serious business and took place in big examination rooms at Rissington Aerodrome.

By far the biggest perk was the chance to fly. Through my close connection with the garage and its R.A.F. clients I could often indulge this pleasure with trusted friends. The first requirement was to obtain a "blood chit"; a form of consent signed by my parents, exonerating the R.A.F. from any responsibility should something awful happen. It was many years later that I realized the tremendous misgivings my mother would have had in signing it. There had been a significant number of fatal accidents by these trainee pilots in our own neighbourhood.

Aircraft accidents are rare nowadays but with so much flying activity in a relatively small area at that time they were fairly common. The local lads, on hearing of yet another, would get on their bikes to go and pick up bits of plane to add to their grisly collections.

I had actually witnessed a couple myself. While working in the garage yard, on hearing a muffled explosion I looked across the valley and watched with awful fascination as the debris from the collision of the two Airspeed Oxfords floated slowly to earth. It came down about three fields north of Great Barrington and quite close to the road. On cycling up to the site I and others were relieved to find that the aircrew involved had already been collected. None survived. The indentations in the soft ground where they'd fallen would always be remembered. Where an arm had been outstretched, even the fingers had left impressions.

At a much later date I was driving on the A40 road and saw a Spitfire crash into woods some two or three miles away. I headed for Eastleach area thinking I might see what had happened. As soon as I turned right up Leys Road I came on a sergeant pilot walking towards me in all his flying gear. Picking him up to take him back to the drome, the chap, very shaken, told me he'd parachuted down after the collision. I told him about the Spitfire but he was quite adamant that they were both Oxfords. I related my story to the guardroom but no notice was taken of me. It was later that my father was covertly informed that there had indeed been found the wreck of a Spitfire exactly where I'd said. The reason for that accident was not known but I have often wondered whether the pilot had lost concentration on witnessing the collision!

Undaunted by these tragedies, I, and the other budding fighter-pilots – all A.T.C. cadets aspired to this – would turn up at "B" Flight office as carefree as could be. On tendering the "blood chit" to the controller in charge, I had but a short wait until an instructor came in for his next pupil. On finding he'd be happy to take me along on his next flight I was fitted with a parachute. These were great heavy things and which, when strapped on, provided a seat for the wearer. Scant time was given to familiarize its recipient with its working.

"When you bale out count five before you pull that thing" – the ripcord.

A short shambling walk to the aircraft, usually an Oxford, but sometimes an Anson. A climb onto the wing root and a duck into the fuselage. The planes were dual control, the instructor on the right and the sometimes apprehensive pupil to his left, me seated just behind. A heady mixture of aircraft dope – the waterproofing applied to the fabric covering wings and fuselage – and high-octane fuel quickly excited the senses.

Most of the instructors were experienced sergeant pilots. This time I was flying with Frank Sparrow, a cheerful Brummie.

The "sprog", as pupils were called, was instructed to go through the usual pre-flight checks and then the engines were coaxed into life. After running them up the brakes were released – only a few years before it would have been "chocks away" – and the plane taxied to the runway. With a deafening roar it accelerated quickly and to a frightening accompaniment of vibration and rattling thumps it reached take-off speed. All of a sudden the wonderful thrill of being airborne took over and all became smooth. The northeast–southwest runway most used overflew a big evergreen plantation, leaving Aldsworth to the right and Ladbarrow Farm to the left. The usual drill was to turn left, make a semi-circle of the airfield and either make an aborted approach or land again. This was "circuits and bumps" and how sometimes they did bump. This time, after a couple of these Frank invited the

This is the actual aircraft which bombed and attached Windrush and was rammed by Bruce Hancock. The photograph shows Unter offizer Rave standing in front of it in Brittany in July 1940.

pupil to let me have a go. He knew that at least I'd already spent a lot of time in "Link Trainers". These were housed in a separate building. They were forerunners of today's virtual reality systems. Mounted on a central pivot, the pupil, in the dark, concentrated on an illuminated display and could simulate the actions of flying an aircraft. Altimeter, level flying horizon, joystick, rudder bars etc as well as physical movement of the trainer were employed in flying it. With two lads, one in the trainer and the other seated watching progress and reactions on another display with a map outside, much "feel" could be achieved. Nevertheless many were the times that the "controller" outside would announce, "That landing was no good, you've just landed fifty feet below ground."

After changing seats with the rather reluctant "sprog" Frank announced, "O.K. Jim, we'll fly over Barrington and Taynton, she's all yours now." What an exhilarating chance, flying over the villages and then at a safe height up Burford High Street! "Now veer left. No, not that fast," as the plane began to crab round. I was soon relieved of my piloting services. The eager pupil was restored to his rightful place and directed to Akeman Street airfield. Here the landing lights were on and as well as the pupil I was given a smoky visor so that I could experience the effect of a night approach. It was unusual to actually land there, so that with a roar of the engines the approach was aborted and the airfield overshot before a return to base.

A nice gesture was made once, when two instructors flew their Oxfords side by side so that Jack Stocks in one, and I in the other one, could wave to each other. Each cadet kept a counter-signed logbook and I clocked up some forty-five hours flying.

Frank Sparrow had a small boxy Jowett car. When the willing, horizontally opposed, little two cylinder engine was motoring on, he described the ride as being like "rattled around like a pea in a bucket". About now the area was assailed by the arrival of American Harvard two-seater trainers. The pupil sat ahead of the instructor. They made an awful racket and seemed accident-prone. They regularly fell out of the sky. The nearest crash was on the approach to Taynton village, but there were too many others as well.

Certain foodstuffs were ever more strictly rationed and those having to exist on those alone must have been hard put to. The country dwellers never really suffered. They could always augment their larders with pigeons, rabbits and hares, with the odd pheasant! Potatoes, turnips and swedes were generally available, as well as their garden produce, together with poultry and pigs, kept in the chicken runs and pigstys at the bottom of the generous kitchen gardens.

My home did well enough. At one time the brush cupboard off my bedroom became home to a whole cheese. That's one heck of a lot of cheese for one family! Though used avidly, it stayed there getting ever more ripe and a large family of mice enjoyed it. My nights were accompanied by furious squeaks and scratching noises. They trailed a copious amount of droppings, which had to be brushed off when more cheese was needed.

Butchers W.J. Castle of Burford, Bill Clack of Eastleach and Bill Pitts of Windrush could usually find "something extra". They were all my father's clients and he kept their delivery vans going.

Sugar presented no problem, even though very strictly rationed. As a beekeeper with some forty hives or so, my father's only hobby, he was allocated a generous ration per hive. This was to feed them through the winter after the season's honey had been extracted. Thus instead of half-pound packets, sugar arrived by the half hundredweight. Father, always too busy to attend properly to his bee hives, left most of them alone, so they kept their honey and had no need for "sugar syrup".

I'd been brought up with regular tablespoonfulls of Cod Liver Oil and Malt. I really liked it but the shops were unable to stock it. But no matter, a generous supply of the treacly malt extract was maintained from lorries refuelling at the garage, whose drivers teased various containers full from their loads. Surprising what does fall off the back of lorries!

Farmers secretly slaughtered pigs, calves and other livestock for their own, and a few discreet friends' tables. Eggs were at a premium and I envied Tom Bartlett, a farmer's son, the six he was said to eat for his breakfasts.

About this time an R.A.F. corporal Giddy came into the post office hoping to find accommodation for his wife and son. They were Londoners who had emerged from their air-raid shelter to find their home practically destroyed, and were desperate to get away. My mother took pity on them and they were duly installed in our large bedroom and big drawing room. The cooking on the old paraffin stoves and other kitchen arrangements had to be shared. She was aghast to discover Mrs Giddy beating her son with a belt and stopped that kind of punishment on pain of eviction.

At about the same time the village received its first batch of evacuee children. They were from London's East End. Now began a difficult period of assimilation. Kids are kids and not always endowed with the finer points of welcome. These poor girls and boys, poor in every sense of the word, were painfully streetwise, sullen and suspicious. They'd obviously had hard lives. They'd been unceremoniously marshalled from an inner city environment and dumped in one which was alien to them. Indeed many of them had never left the city before. Their appearance contrasted absolutely with the local kids. Pale complexions, sparse, near white hair and their poor little limbs, marked them out. They later achieved a more ruddy look and filled out accordingly.

They brought with them and taught the local children strange and incomprehensible songs, with the result that kids would run around, happily singing them, one of which ended:

"And if you don't come
I'll tickle your bum
With a lump of celery."

I never did know where we were supposed to come to.
Another –   I don't want to join the army
             I don't want to go to war
             I'd sooner hang around
             Piccadilly Underground
             Living on the earnings
             Of a highborn lady.

Mrs Giddy and son later returned to London and their space was filled with my aunt and her son from East Barnet. They gave way to Squadron Leader Heelas and his wife, who delighted in annoying him by suddenly declaring things like "Joe, do you know your left ear is much lower than the right one." He'd get quite upset and his carefully cultivated moustache would really bristle. These moustaches were "de rigueur" for R.A.F. flying crew. He was never very impressed when his wife attended functions with his Wing Commander instead of him, especially when she wore a bracelet given by that same gentleman. They had a Rover 14, which he kept in immaculate condition. His family owned the large Heelas store in Reading and with help from my father's surfeit of petrol coupons, he was able to visit them regularly.

A Sergeant Duffy and his wife lived in Rose Cottage, Little Barrington (where Charles Sollis now lives). He would regale his friends with tales of rural life and how he had to bury the contents of the Elsan – a kind of chemical assisted, bucket loo – in his garden, which he named "The Petunia Patch". In civilian life he retired and became landlord of the Chequers Inn at Kencot. In the bar he displayed some of the wartime notices, which abounded in the various messes. One such read:

A wise old owl sat in an oak
The more he heard the less he spoke
The less he spoke the more he heard
Airmen you should imitate that bird.

Windrush aerodrome was farmland commandeered from the Sherborne Estate. One young "gentle-man" tenant farmer, Roy Berry, who as a consequence lost many of his acres, was unmarried and lived with his very sophisticated but gentle mother in Le Mary farmhouse at Windrush. He mixed easily with the public school element in the officer fraternity and seemed to spend more time and money in the officer's mess than was good for him. One day a phone call to the garage found my father and me searching for Roy's Triumph Gloria motor car in one of his fields by the road leading to the 'drome. This became a more difficult hunt than might be supposed. With one of his inspirations he had recently "repainted" this attractive motorcar with a distinctive coat of golden distemper. He'd left the farm track and driven into his own field of long-stemmed barley. In the dark and after numerous forays into the "unknown", he'd abandoned it and called for help the next morning. It wasn't easy to distinguish it even in daylight.

Perhaps inevitably, although as a farmer in a reserved occupation, he'd succumbed to the allure and thrill of the boys in blue – the Brylcreem Boys – he'd volunteered as an officer cadet. Soon after being commissioned he married a W.R.A.F. officer. He lost his life in action. His grief stricken mother awakened the sympathies of the locality. Her plight was heightened when it became known that Roy's widow claimed everything in the house and left his mother with next to nothing. She had to vacate the farm soon after.

In the fullness of time I celebrated my 17th birthday. To me, by far the most important gift was the brand new driving licence I obtained that day. As a wartime measure driving tests were suspended. When they were eventually re-introduced, anyone having held a provisional one for more than a year before that date was automatically issued with a full one and avoided any test whatsoever. My father was likewise overjoyed because he then found his son could begin to generate more revenue. I was then allocated ASR850, a 1938 Austin 10 saloon for which I became responsible, not only as the driver, but also the maintenance man.

The taxi work that I did began in a relatively orderly manner. Private car fuel allowances diminished and were eventually suspended. Hire cars had a special allowance and with that, copiously supplemented by more from the garage surplus, our cars had no restriction in use.

Then it was ruled that taxis and hire cars would be limited to operate solely within a ten-mile radius of their base. This ruled out any competition from the Oxford, Cheltenham or Swindon areas. By the same token, local railway stations and the infrequent buses were the only escapes from this area. These became remarkably busy; Kingham Station was used by the R.A.F. while Shipton-under-Wychwood was the nearest for the locals.

Basil Howse's bus, from Aldsworth, an old Bedford, provided transport to and from Cheltenham station. He'd meet the late Sunday evening train and returned, often packing nearly as many standing as seated. Unlike the modern coach, which has ample luggage stowage, accessed by lifting big-hinged panels below the seating area, his bus was equipped with a long luggage rack along the rooftop. This was reached by means of a metal ladder bolted to the rear of the vehicle. He'd often notice that she'd seem top heavy and laboured more than usual and guessed that there were stowaways aboard. These, despite inclement weather, had climbed up on the rack and were braving the elements, either because the bus was full or to avoid paying the fare. He voiced his genuine concern that he was always worried that, passing through the tunnel as he came up Tunnel Hill beyond Andoversford, they might be maimed or even killed. The tunnel was excavated away soon after the war.

I was called on for numerous journeys from Rissington Aerodrome to Kingham Station and back, picking up my clients from the guard room at the main gate. I was also issued with a pass which allowed me to proceed to the very imposing Officers' Mess. The Sergeants' Mess was opposite the Guard Room and over the years my parents were invited to many of its functions. Though they rarely took a drink, it was renowned for its bibulous entertainment.

Shipton station is nearest to the village and was its escape to the outside world. Its platform sign read, "Shipton for Burford". The railway moguls had wanted to lay their track directly to Burford but the landowners of the day would not countenance such an invasion of their property. Hence it diverted to Shipton. One of my regular passengers was Colonel Wingfield of Barrington Park. He seemed unable to realise that my small car was unable to cover the ground as fast as his large chauffeur driven limousines and was invariably late emerging from his great mansion. I did my best, but sometimes on breasting the top of Shipton Downs, the telltale smoke of the approaching train could be seen and so a quick dash to Charlbury was needed. A couple of times when the train was about to leave the platform the guard spotted our arrival and held the train for him. This was always seen to be worth a handsome tip.

More villagers were 'called up' and others volunteered for service. Margaret Griffin, the miller's younger daughter, had been helping my father out with the taxi work. She was good and let nothing worry her. This stopped when she joined the A.T.S. (Auxiliary Territorial Service) and soon became a staff car driver. Mary Dowthwaite, whose father had quite recently taken over the mill, on the death of Charles Griffin, had joined the F.A.N.Y's, (First Aid Nursing Yeomanry). Her father was the last tenant to operate the Barrington Mill.

Then, to the astonishment of the whole village, Laura Davis, who lived at home, looking after her totally blind mother, received her call-up papers. She was directed into the W.A.A.F. (Womens' Auxiliary Air Force). A compromise was reached and she was stationed at Little Rissington. Tiny though she was, she had to cycle through all weathers, back and forth, between her duties and her commitment at home. Tom Townsend also joined the R.A.F., spending much of his time manning the pillbox guarding the southern approach to the aerodrome.

The impressive Barrington Village Hall came to life. Many concerts and dances were attended and organized by R.A.F. personnel who were only too pleased to get out of camp. There was a core of professionals among them; Ronnie Pleydell, a big band leader, as well as several music hall acts.

The odd visit by German aircraft was heralded, if the wind was in the right direction, by the Burford air-raid siren. It was installed at The Tolsey. This scary din had small effect. Unlike the towns and cities where all had access to a communal shelter or their own garden boltholes, little notice was taken. It was generally agreed that if your name wasn't on a bomb it wouldn't get you and "it's always the one you don't hear that does".

Cruel jokes were made about the school headmaster, Mr. Gibbs. He was smitten by an awful fear. At night he drove his little Austin car up onto Shipton Downs where he found some sense of security. Without doubt he'd have been just as safe at home in his own bed, in his wife's company. Maybe he'd have found a smile had he talked to old Jim Tidmarsh, who persisted in talking about "Old Ilter". Jim probably got just the same perverse kick out of this mispronunciation as my father did later, who still after many corrections, persisted in continuing to call the Allied Supreme Commander, "Eisenhouser".

I had by now become quite used to a double working life. The busy life of car repair was constantly interrupted by calls for taxi work. My Austin was doing a valiant job but when a bigger car was needed my father was there with his "Floating Power" Citroen limousine. This really was a capacious vehicle. As well as the two generous seats in the front and a three seater at the back, it was blessed with two occasional ones, which could fold into the floor space between. There was no rear boot, but a large wooden box was bolted onto the car's substantial luggage rack. This car had been owned by Colonel Hurst of Little Barrington Grove, who owned half of the village, as well as extensive lands to the south of the River Windrush right through to Burford. Petrol rationing had caused him to look for a smaller vehicle. This need was solved when my father struck a deal for the Citroen against a very nice black Ford saloon. This arrangement suited them both.

Soon the status quo was to be mightily interrupted!

CHAPTER THREE

The Yanks Arrive

One summer night the peace and quiet of the village and my own slumbers were shattered. My bedroom window overlooked the war memorial, which stands at the junction of the village roads. There was a sound of heavy traffic. Strange voices were heard directing the drivers of a constant stream of big vehicles. Hand held torches and hooded headlights lit up the scene.

No, not a German invasion; the Yanks had arrived.

I feel that I should now declare and point out that I could fall foul of today's politically correct and anti-racist brigades, but I believe the reporting of events and attitudes more than sixty years ago needs to be recorded. **These attitudes should not apply now.**

The tide of unfamiliar vehicles and smartly uniformed soldiers seemed endless.

When things had settled down it was established that the Deer Park was now home to some six thousand white American Air Force Engineers and their impressive equipment. Their main task on getting to Europe would be to carve out and prepare landing strips for their Air Force. Such massive machinery had never been seen before. Diamond T transporters; D8 and D4 Caterpillar tractors; graders; diggers and levellers abounded.

Initially they used the Park entrance behind which the village cricket pitch had existed for ages and then another gateway to the left of the road down to the Manor Farm. They were all confined to camp for the first few days. During this time they pitched hundreds of tents, completely destroyed the cricket pitch and laid paths over and beyond it.

The top entrance was opposite an area known as Quarry Banks. It was from these workings that so much of the building stone had been quarried for the houses and stone walls around us. They soon employed their machines to reduce all these grass grown hillocks and trenches to a few roods of level vehicle park. This was their "motor pool". The farm sheep dip just there made an excellent inspection and grease pit.

Now ensued a mad era for the village and for my father and me in particular. I was just seventeen years old and would not be eligible for conscription until my eighteenth birthday. On top of all the struggle to keep the busy garage and taxi business going we became overwhelmed by this influx of GI's, as American troops were called – short for Government Issue.

Our home, also the village Post Office, backed onto the war memorial with its encircling low walls and road junctions. The GI's only had to leave camp to be there. This became the pick up point for the local 'Cabs'. As soon as they were allowed out it became obvious they only had two goals – to find some drink and "a cute piece of ass". Because of the existing ten mile radius for hire cars this became difficult. Essentially there were only three cabs available, our two and Mr. Lake with his smart Vauxhall 14 from Bourton. Armies of very thirsty and love-starved GI's descended on the war memorial, demanding to be transported, usually to Bourton. While waiting, they would play ever more serious games of "craps", the losers, often enough, having to go back to camp. A charge of half a crown a head to or from Bourton was settled on.

Some sort of working order had to be developed. I left my father's garage at 4.30pm for my tea-time. Because there were always GI's waiting for me on the road side of our house, I had to park my car in Lock's orchard and rush quickly over two paddocks to the front door without being seen;

have my tea, back into the car and be ready for the impossible scrabble that usually ensued. Now, we have a small-medium size saloon car. How many bodies could it reasonably contain? Two in the front beside the driver, three squashed along the rear seat and two more sitting on them. Eight in a four seater, another GI knocking furiously on the window,

"Jimmy, me and my pals next time, we'll walk to meet you."

"OK, won't be long."

Down to Bourton, turn round, meet the next ones, turn round, and meet the next group. And so it was, backwards and forwards all evening. The half-crown a head and none ever failed to come round to the driver, even in the darkest and wettest of weathers. By now my father had closed the garage and was playing a similar role.

The "last" load down to Bourton would be about 9 pm. By this time the earlier ones would opt to come back and would be first of the many trips in reverse. This punishing existence, seven days a week, took its inevitable toll on this seventeen year old. It became difficult to stay awake despite the colourful repartee around me. Many were the times that I would nod off, especially when on my own, only to wake when a front wheel hit the road-verge. Thank goodness there was zero traffic around. Sometimes I would spit on my finger, moisten my eyes and open the car door window to incline my head so that the cold air could keep me awake. Several times when my mother, being worried that I was particularly late, would come into the yard and find me fast asleep over the steering wheel.

The long "hikes", route marches to us, took the GI's to many other remote villages. I found myself being directed to them and their pubs, The Farmers Arms at Cold Aston, The Black Horse in Naunton to name a couple. Barrington pubs usually kept their doors locked most of the time. Locals would be let in through the back way. Beer and spirits were in such short supply that a bottle of whiskey, price, ten shillings and sixpence, could fetch seven pounds if any could be acquired.

Postcard of Great Barringtion War Memorial and rear of our house

At this time there were other white GI's at Sherborne. Shipton-under-Wychwood and Shipton Court premises were host to a black American unit. The white GI's and the black ones were strictly separated. The white ones were overwhelmingly anti-black. During my months with them I learnt many Americanisms. Most informative sentences ended with, "I ain't shitting. I ain't a bird-turding," but the worst expletives were reserved for the "goddam jiggerboos".

"Jimmy, don't you never have nuttin to do with them goddam black bastards" etc. They were never seen in our area and the white ones were prohibited from going to Shipton.

At this time, young and not so very young women camp followers came on the scene, some of them renting attics and back rooms wherever possible.

As was the case the country over, liaisons were formed between the troops and local females and who could blame them? This revelation will come as no surprise to later generations. As is well quoted, "The Yanks are overpaid, oversexed and over here." They could afford to treat the English girls, who had already struggled with the rigours of rationing and the unavailability of clothing, to luxuries some had never seen. Cartons of Lucky Strike, Camel and Philip Morris cigarettes were the common coinage and sheer silk stockings scored with the ladies. To complement all this, the smart uniforms and the American accent, only previously heard in picture houses, (cinemas), really tipped the balance. I was asked,

"Jimmy, ain't you got a sister?"

"Me? Yes, but she's too young, only fifteen."

"Well, if they're big enough, they're old enough."

In my innocence I didn't take that seriously but had no cause to worry.

Inevitably when they were "long gone", babies arrived. In that era, babies born out of wedlock caused devastating problems for their mothers. To the outsiders most would go unnoticed, but the children of the black American units, like those at Shipton, proclaimed their origins.

I always liked the American troops and so have always felt an affinity with the American people. I got to know my regular taxi fares and would sometimes miss a familiar face. The conversation would go like this:

"Where's Chuck today?"

"He's in the stockade, came back late off furlough. They gave him seven days and busted him."

The stockade was the guardroom and "busted him" meant he'd had his stripes taken away. He'd now be back as a "buck private".

The unfamiliar ranks were soon understood. There were PFCs, (Private First Class), Buck Sergeants, Tech Sergeants, Top Sergeants, Master Sergeants and so on. The stripes were worn upside down as far as the British Army was concerned.

I regularly took a colonel to a large country house to pay his respects to the lady, whose husband was commanding troops abroad. Another officer visited the house which is now Lloyds Bank in Bourton. Naturally they had the cab to themselves and expected a degree of discretion.

When fully loaded the poor little car sagged so much at the rear that the tyres fouled the mudguards. So Bill Hall, the village blacksmith, was called on to set the springs up. Each spring leaf was heated and hammered to achieve a more elliptical shape and when refitted, the car was a good six inches higher. Most of the floor insulating rubbers had broken away with the result that as the car splashed through puddles, sprays of muddy water shot up inside. The unfortunate N.A.A.F.I. manageress from Windrush aerodrome was taken regularly to Burford Bank and took these hardships in good spirit.

Numerous adventures ensued from this taxi work.

One day, having just taken a full load to Bourton, I got within half a mile of base when I met a lone GI. He stood, waving his arms, in the middle of the road, forcing me to stop, even though I knew many more were waiting. He waved fistfuls of money in my face and offered me anything to take him back to The Lamb at Rissington. I did. It transpired that he had won six hundred and forty pounds at "crap", a huge amount then and worth at least fifteen thousand pounds today. He enjoyed one hell of an evening, got blind drunk, was picked up by the "Snowdrops" (Military Police) and thrown into the stockade, his unspent winnings still intact!

Another time, nearly 1am, I made my last run to Bourton. The local police sergeant was there waiting with a group of GI's. Having filled the car he said,

"You'll be coming back for the rest?"

On my telling him I'd had enough, he said, "We'll get them all in now, come on lads."

By dint of much shouting and shoving he did, closing the rear door by putting an ample shoulder against it, and outside, the quite substantial boot-lid was pulled down and two more bodies rode back on it. Coming up the hill in Rissington the exhaust pulled apart, the din was horrendous. It seems the over laden chassis must have flexed, so sliding the front pipe out of the silencer. The impossible count on getting back to camp was eleven GI's transported. They needed unfolding when they staggered out.

One evening when halfway back to Bourton, I met my father. We passed slowly enough for him to shout that he had got the last ones. It was some sight. The faithful old Citroen sported wide running boards – the car mounting step running between the front and rear wings. There were two GI's standing on each of them, two squeezed into the big wooden luggage box and twelve others inside. No one else knew, but the old cable brakes were so bad from the lack of time and spares to repair them, that the old man sometimes had to drag the wheels along the nearside grass bank verges to stop. No wonder, at times like this, with eighteen passengers!

Another time, my innocence and lack of knowledge of the fair sex was severely tried. I was picking up a group of five from outside The Old New Inn at Bourton.

"Just wait a minute Jimmy, Red won't be long."

Red did appear from the garden opposite and I was fascinated to hear the lurid accounts of how each had performed with the same lady of little virtue down in the shrubbery. Red had caught hold of her by the ears and been subjected to a pastime I could hardly guess at. Then I was told,

"Jeez Jimmy, we'll hang on while you go and grab a piece."

Never did I move that car so quickly!

Coming back one day I came upon a sorry sight. There was Mr. Lake from Bourton, surrounded by several GI's. His shiny, immaculate Vauxhall stood on the road enmeshed in telephone wires. Not the swiftest of drivers, he was being overtaken by a Jeep. The problem was that the GI driver tried to pass on the nearside and hit a telegraph pole so hard that it snapped and fell across the car, hence the wires everywhere. The poor man, determined to make someone pay, spent much time taking all the relevant particulars. Unhappily, as he later told me, the Jeep was "proven" to have been stolen by another unit and he'd wasted his time.

After months of this close contact, I found I was able to tell where so many of them came from, the Southern drawl, the laconic sounds of the Mid-West and the spics from "Noo York" were all there. But all, and I mean all, were gentlemen to this innocent country boy.

"Have a cee-gar Jimmy."

And a handful would be thrust into my lap. Surprisingly, I didn't smoke in those days but have more than made up for it since.

All these men generated an awful amount of effluent. To deal with this, several small flatbed trucks were used. They were based at Fosters Garage, Burford. The big double entry doors to it now give access to a part of what is now the Oxford Shirt Company. With shallow tailboard and sides, they were laden with open-topped barrels and dustbins. Their function was to be filled with excrement, which they emptied over a big field on Shipton Downs, the opposite side of the road from the wood, which now has a mobile phone mast. There it lay, stinking. On the many times I drove to Shipton, my passengers and I tried desperately to close the windows and hold our breath. The smell would even have invaded a modern car but our old ones were hopeless. It hung around so long!

Far more worrying was that, as these trucks left camp to journey to Shipton Downs, they turned the sharp corner by the war memorial, which caused them to sway. This resulted in a generous amount of their load being tipped sideways and splashing out onto the road resulting in great turds rolling around and much liquid in streams.

On occasion, the unfortunates waiting around for a cab and playing "craps" would be treated to some of their own back. Oh dear!

As a mechanic I was well aware that the chaps in Fosters Garage deserved every penny that they were paid for servicing the lorries. I had only to deal with the butchers and milk delivery vehicles where the wooden floors reeked to high heaven despite all efforts to clean them.

There was also a huge quantity of discarded food and general rubbish to get rid of. Most of this ended up in a quarry at the top of the Steeps. This is on the road just out of Bourton leading to Sherborne. Many people will have seen televised scenes of beggars in poor countries scavenging waste dumps; similar activities could have been recorded at that quarry. Having heard of the bounty available, I called to see for myself. One man was living on site in a crude hut, a number of others prodded around and waited for the next lorry load. As it was disgorged, it was eagerly fallen upon. I understood that unopened food cans could be found as well as other "treasures". An awful stench pervaded the area, that of rotting food, and flies were attracted in swarms. One look was enough for me. Later, when they prepared to exit for D-Day, they dumped a stack of useful material in a small quarry just below Great Rissington cricket ground. As I passed that way so often, I was able to stop and rescue such items as vehicle stands, metal workbenches etc.

In October came this news, which shocked the village. I write it as reported in The Burford Courier:

Official information has been received by Mr. and Mrs. L. Hands, that their son, Sergeant P. Leslie Hands (aged 19), a Flight Engineer in the R.A.F.V.R. has been killed in action. Leslie had completed flight operations with Bomber Command; he had flown over Germany on many occasions and was always a very efficient member of a grand crew. The story begins when the bomber, in which Leslie was a member, took off and successfully flew over Germany's industrials towns. The plane reached the English coast safely, then disaster awaited them, for a sneak German fighter aircraft followed them home. The result was the bomber was shot down and it crashed to the ground, killing all the crew who had completed the task they were sent out to do.

> The pains of death are past
> Labour and sorrow cease
> And life's long warfare closed at last
> His soul is found in peace.

He had attended school at Great Barrington and Northleach Grammar (with me).

The funeral took place on October 2nd; the R.A.F. padre conducted it. Rissington airmen fired a salute in tribute and the Last Post was sounded; a day I will never forget! To make it even worse, as I was driving some of the Hands family, following the hearse and about to cross the bridge by The Fox Inn towards Great Barrington, a big American truck was coming fast towards us. The driver, suddenly realising the gravity of the situation, slammed all his brakes on. There was a resounding crunch from the rear, the GI's leapt from the back and pushed a very broken Jeep, with steam everywhere, into the field before they were able to back up and clear the bridge.

The village had already known tragedy. Mr. Mervyn Wingfield, eldest son of Colonel Wingfield, owner of Great Barrington Park Estate, was also killed while flying training at Calgary in Canada. His brother, Charles, sustained a serious head wound while serving as an army commissioned officer in France.

To add to these tragedies, young "Wunner" Forest of Burford, with whom I had become friends in the A.T.C., was killed in combat. He had been one of the star cadets. He left school to work at

Leafield. This unit, best known locally as Langley Poles, because of its proliferation of tall inter-linked radio masts, was an important international communication centre. He became skilled at sending and receiving messages in Morse Code and put all other A.T.C. cadets to shame, when struggling with all the dots and dashes. I found that sending was so much easier than receiving, and have never forgotten the code, which might just have come in useful later on.

He became the envy of all the boys when he joined the R.A.F. and achieved their absolute goal, a Spitfire pilot. To thrill them all he "shot up" Burford High Street in his Spitfire on a number of occasions. The old Burford families felt his loss very keenly.

Besides the collections of every bit of aluminium, treasured pots and pans which were needed to manufacture aircraft, the public were asked to contribute towards their cost. Small towns like Burford, pledged to fund a Spitfire. To demonstrate its progress and inform us all as to how we were doing, The Tolsey erected a large placard showing a barometer. It was inspiring to watch it climb steadily to reach the huge target of £5,000, the cost of the aircraft. For those, now unaware, The Tolsey also housed the fire engine, and appliances as well as the air raid warning siren.

We nowadays worry about "Weapons of Mass Destruction". Nothing changes! In October '43 The Courier made this announcement:

WILL IT BE CHEMICAL WARFARE?

Although Mr. Schicklgruber has not yet turned on the gas, one never knows when he will release it over our Isles.

"What about your gas mask?"

"Don't leave it any old place out of hand."

Then follows a warning by Number 4 (Witney area) Civil Defence:

"You are responsible for the gas mask issued to you. Get it fitted properly."

Burford also adopted a warship, "H.M.S. Aldenham", and its photograph was displayed in the Misses Wickins' shop window. All members of the crew signed it. Plaques presented to Burford, Upton and Signett were also on view. These were signed by the Lord Commissioners of The Admiralty, to commemorate the adoption of H.M.S. Aldenham during "warship week" which was held in March 1943.

Another great friend, William Arkell, son of Mr. Fred Arkell, of Barrington Park Farm, joined the Fleet Air Arm on November 1st 1943. He returned from service to take on the farm. One of his most memorable feats of "modernization" was to plant a potato crop in a water meadow, next

The "City of Oxford" paid by the money donated by the people of Oxfordshire

to the River Windrush. This enabled him to use modern spray equipment, but the super abundant crop was never harvested. A very rainy season caused the river to flood the field, which rotted all of it. Soon after this he formed a consortium with two other young farmers and emigrated to Western Australia. There, after much "prairie busting" with massive machines, he was unlucky enough to be hit by one of that country's droughts; trial by fire and water! He survived, very successfully.

It has to be acknowledged that all the feverish activity by father and son in our business generated a lot of pound notes! I am writing this account on my late father's knee-hole desk. He started to fill one drawer with these notes, in orderly rows. When one drawer was full, another was started. He gave me a quarter of my takings and I proceeded to do the same in "my drawer". Neither of us had any idea how much was there. Suffice it to say, Lloyds Bank never saw any of it, nor did the tax man!

Father never did believe in banks. My stash was still growing until the day I was "called up". At this point, my mother put a few pounds a week into my savings account, during my three years away. My father never ever spent anything and continued to work all hours for the rest of his working life.

This money became something of a liability. Being used notes, it smelt and went mouldy. Over the years that followed, bundles of it had to be changed when each new issue came out. He even kept some in his beehives, some he changed into silver coinage. This was very heavy and later on, my mother related that, when the estate workmen had to do work in the attic of our house, there was a big tin trunk to move. One asked her,

"Whatever is in there, is it full of money?"

Some mouldered away after he had buried it in a tin box. The lesson here is that, had he banked and paid tax, its value would have been enhanced over the years instead of depreciating through inflation.

His accountant, Mr. F.G. Jones of Stow, had a hopeless task. Indeed, when I inherited the business, he said,

"I hope you'll be better than your father. He was one of the few people who were never investigated and now, after seven years, he's got away with it."

Of course, I declared every penny, and who wouldn't!

Now came some more shocking news. Poor Fred Sweet, head gardener for the big house, having nurtured his impressive cordon trained peaches, was devastated when some GI had the temerity to climb the kitchen garden wall and appropriate them. Such vandalism was unique!

Back at the garage, things muddled on, even fewer spare parts. Winter began to set in with all its difficulties. Most work was done in an open yard, with only a jury-rigged sheet to ward off the rain and snow.

Lying under cars, with rivulets of water running through and in sub-zero conditions, an old Beatrice paraffin stove was used to warm the tools on. By this time, Edward Ball, whose father was general factotum for Miss Wilbraham of Church Farm, had started as a fourteen-year-old apprentice.

Fordson Standard tractors needed much repair work; their big problem was clutch failure. This meant splitting them in two. The clutch was a multi-plate, the plates, some dozen or so, were made of sprung steel and dished. All bolted together and installed, the clutch pedal required hefty leg muscles to depress it. Often enough, the tractor would come to a halt in the middle of a field that was being ploughed, and there it had to be repaired, in a slough of wet mud. I so often blamed the war for making my life so hard.

I'd left Grammar School with a very decent School Certificate, nearly all credits, with French my only failure. This must have been a particular disappointment to my mother. She loved to intersperse her conversation with apt French phrases. She also took a French grammar class at home for which local children paid a few pennies. Sadly, at my very young age, I rebelled against it and it had a negative effect on me.

Douglas C47 Dakota

On leaving school I would probably have been able to pursue further education and maybe an academic career. The diplomatic corps could have been my goal. Unfortunately, wartime problems dictated otherwise. My eventual fate was, without doubt, a "grease monkey". Planning ahead seemed so impractical, the only certainty being that the call to King and country would come.

The winter of '43 came and went, then in late Spring of '44 obvious preparations for what was to become known as D-Day, were sensed.

All the American vehicles were systematically waterproofed. Jeeps, lorries and transporters began to boast aerial exhausts and air intake pipes. Great quantities of heavy, greasy water proofing compound was spread and smeared over the electronics to protect them from the seawater of a beach landing. To test their efficiency, each one was driven through a man-made water filled channel. This was on the Sherborne to Farmington road, on the right hand side, just before the turn up to the A40.

The "hikes" which the GI's took became more demanding.

I had by this time volunteered for enlistment in the R.A.F.V.R. for aircraft duties. The original letter in reply, I have before me, dated 1st April 1944, telling me to report at 0.900 hours to R.A.F. section, Combined Services Recruiting Centre, Shoe Lane, New Inn Hall Street, Oxford and to take my Air Training Corps certificates. If accepted, I was to return home to await my orders. The worry this must have caused my family was not recognised by their seventeen and a half year old son.

Meanwhile, the R.A.F. had developed and occupied a new airfield at Broadwell on the Bradwell Grove estate. It was originally intended for the use of American 8th Air Force, but with a change of plan the R.A.F. arrived on 2nd February 1944 and opened it to Numbers 512 and 525 squadron of Dakotas. They were to act as freighters, troop carriers, ambulances and glider tugs. They did several exercises with troops of the 1st Landing Brigade in April. Just before D-Day, all the Dakotas were painted with black and white stripes on their wings and fuselage to aid in recognition.

After a delay, because of unfavourable weather, some one thousand troops boarded the transport at 10 pm and the signal to go was given to Wing Commander Coventry of 512 Squadron at 11.15pm. He took off, followed by the rest of the squadron, thirty-two aircraft in all. Next followed 525 Squadron, led by Wing Commander Jefferson, they were all air-borne by 11.35pm and struck out for the Channel coast and France. After dropping their paratroops over the dropping zones they were back at base for mid-day.

They then prepared for a second operation, this time towing Horsa gliders in daylight, in an operation codenamed "Mallard". Thirty-seven aircraft from both squadrons, watched over by fighter planes, made successful drops, but lost one, which came down in the Channel with engine failure. For several days after 7th June, they dropped supplies, food, water, ammunition and medical supplies for the advancing troops. They continued with support operations and also flew the wounded back.

Then in September they made ready for another operation codenamed "Market Garden". This was to be the ill-fated Arnhem landings, designed to capture the Rhine river bridges. A number of Dakotas, their Horsa gliders and their crews were lost, but support activities continued until the end of the campaign.

This kind of work went on until the German surrender on the 6th May 1945. These aircraft were then moved on and other Dakota squadrons moved in. They re-equipped and moved to the Far East where the Japanese were still fighting. Then on the 5th October 1945, 271 Squadron flew in and continued the duties within Transport Command, before being disbanded on 1st December 1946, well after the end of the war. Their drinking song, (learnt also by the locals), was:

There's old Wing Co. Peters
He raves and he shouts
He shouts about things he knows FA about
Fly high; fly low, wherever you go
271 Squadron will never say no.

Douglas C47 Dakota, this plane is part of the
320 Squadron based at Broadwell

The prototype Airspeed Horsa glider. This was the main
troop carrying glider of the scond world war. (Crown)

CHAPTER FOUR

The Reluctant Squaddy

In Barrington it was now Spring '44 and all of a sudden, overnight, no GI's. The camp had enforced a ban on any movement outside its limits. A few of the troops did take a very considerable risk to say goodbye to their girlfriends, and then they were gone; every man and vehicle, leaving a total vacuum. It was guessed they'd moved out to "somewhere" for an invasion somewhere and some time.

The grinding and wearisome business of taxi work became manageable, though there was still plenty with locals and R.A.F. personnel. Then, a few days later, I was returning from Bourton, on top of the Steeps, when a once in a lifetime spectacle caused me to stop. From this vantage point it seemed the whole sky was filled with aircraft and gliders on tow. They collected right there in front of me, from every point of the compass, circling round and round, until, on a given signal, they flew south in an endless stream astern. The invasion of Europe had been enthusiastically received, so it was obvious where they were heading. This was D-Day plus one.

Soon afterwards, I was contacted to take overnight kit to Oxford, from where, with others, to go to Ad Astral House, London, for my final R.A.F. interviews and tests. By the second afternoon I found myself one of only a dozen survivors from one hundred and twenty, who were deemed to be worthy of pilot training. Then, at the conclusion of a strict medical examination, I was given a test for colour blindness. This started by showing me pages in a book, which were covered in coloured dots. I had to read off numbers, which showed up quite distinctly as darker dots. Having read off a couple or three, the next page was blank, so were some others. I naturally said so, but wondered why they had bothered. I was then informed that my sight was suspect and placed at the end of a dark tunnel to name lights switched on consecutively at the other end. I struggled to identify them and was then informed, with some compassion, that I had failed. Until then I had been quite unaware of the problem. I then got desperate and volunteered for any flying duty, even the dreaded tail-gunner, to no effect at all. It was explained that I could jeopardize the whole crew if asked to identify a beacon light and gave a wrong report.

It must have been a great relief to my parents, when a very dejected son came home to report failure, and to be resigned to call-up.

Even call-up to the Army was not a certainty; an evil lottery of names would see one youth in every ten, as they became eligible for service, eighteen years old, directed to the coal-mines. They were called Bevan Boys, after Aneurin Bevan, the Cabinet Minister, who perpetrated this outrage.

It is still difficult to imagine what these lads went through. To be snatched from remote country villages and forced to work underground in a coal-pit, located in some already hostile environment, must have been absolute hell.

On 24th July 1944, confirmation of my non-acceptance as air crew was received, the rather curt letter ended with, "you will, in due course, be called up for service in the Army."

Then on the 8th August I received the unwelcome news that I must report to Norton Barracks, Worcester on the 17th August. A railway warrant was included from Shipton Station to Worcester. After another working week, Father drove me to catch the designated train; my army career had begun.

Worcester, nowadays so near, seemed a world away.

Arriving there, it then became obvious that I'd been in the company of many other callow youths, who descended on the platform. We were immediately herded together by several smart soldiers and directed to get into one of those high-bodied army lorries. A short drive through the town and we entered the imposing confines of the Regimental Barracks.

It was a fine, sunny day and the regimental band was out on the greensward to welcome us. Their chosen music was the war-time song,

This is the Army Mr. Brown
You and your lady went to town
She had you worried but this is war
And she won't worry you any more

Do what the bugler demands
He's in the Army and not in the band
You had your breakfast in bed before
But you won't get it there any more

"Come on, hurry up there, pick up your cases and get in line."

For the shambolic and sorry looking recruits, this was the first of the thousands of orders they would get during their Army life. A roll-call, name to be answered audibly and then a disorderly trudge to a hutment.

"Right, get inside and find a bed and get back out here."

"Come on, you should be out again by now".

The next goal was the quartermaster's stores. Faced by a long wooden-counter, the new soldiers to be were appraised by one of several Q.M's staff standing behind it. They were supposed to be able to issue clothing that would fit without even the use of a tape measure. Working along from one end, it was;

"Denims, one, blouses, one, trousers, one, vests, two, housewife, one", and so on down to, "Army blankets, two, mess tin, one" etcetera. Overloaded with all this strange kit, it was back to the hut to try it on and sort things out.

In charge of the hut were one sergeant who bunked elsewhere, a corporal and a lance corporal who enjoyed the privacy of a small room walled off at the end of the hut.

"Right, outside and get to the cookhouse. Bring your mess tins."

These aluminium tins were [some] 6" x 4" in shape, shallow and with a long, double-wired, swivel handle. This allowed the tin to be carried by folding it back so it would slide down behind the army belt.

As the line progressed through the cookhouse, each picked up a mess plate, which was then assailed by a dubious looking meal. At the end of the line the mess tin was held out for some army tea. I'd never had to drink tea at home, didn't like it, getting by on coffee, cocoa or plain water. Really didn't like it all, but realising that there was no alternative and I'd need some liquid, I took some.

The mess tin, being so wide and shallow, cooled it in no time. It slopped over and around it and defied most efforts to raise it and drink from one corner. The taste was strange, unlike any previously encountered tea and certainly contained lots of Bromide, the army way of suppressing sexual activity. Contrary to the complaints of the others, I found it at least palatable. Having dealt with the squalid mess at table, exit was by way of the rear of the canteen, past large containers into which all uneaten food was scraped. They didn't look good, smelt terrible, and, being August, attracted more than their fair share of wasps and flies; so much uneaten food found its way there.

Back to the hut, more sorting out and a first lesson in bed-making. First lay the paliasse on the unforgiving, metal strip bed base, and then a couple of rough army blankets, one to sleep on the other one to cover. Oh dear, what with the terrible discomfort of the harsh blankets and the noisy, smelly company of the others, I found sleeping difficult and shed the odd tear into my pillow.

I dropped off eventually, but was woken at 6 a.m. by the very noisy lance corporal shouting, "Come on you lot, hands off your cocks, eyes on your socks, outside now in your gym kit."

This was nothing but a vest and a pair of blue shorts.

After a spell of stretching and jumping around, it was, "Right, inside and get changed. Come on, you ought to be out by now, last man out to report to me later."

Some sight we were! The uniforms fitted where they touched and the hob-nailed boots were agony on the feet.

After breakfast – reconstituted egg and burnt bacon –

"Right, haircut."

We were marched to where, on this summers' day, three chairs were standing on the grass. With much protest and under attack from three "barbers", all were given "short back and sides" army fashion. Those who objected lost most hair.

Back to the hut, where instruction was given on how to assemble the equipment, small pack, big pack, water bottle, various straps and a belt. The use of the button stick was demonstrated, it being slid behind the brass buttons and buckles to keep the Brasso from contact with the garments. The heavy, stiff leather boots were then treated to the first of many applications of "Dubbing". This had to be rubbed in to preserve and soften the leather.

All of these jobs were both messy and onerous. Little did the lads realise that soon after the boots had taken on a dull and greasy look, the parade inspection would call for them to be highly polished. The big, round studs in the boot soles were counted, thirteen to each boot. In the parades to come, each man would have to lift his feet so that the inspecting officer, by now walking behind the ranks, could check them. A stud missing could mean extra duties. A usual trick was to carry a couple of spare studs and push them into the holes left by the lost ones.

By this time, I had realised that I and a farm boy from the Chilterns, (Wycombe), were the only country lads. The others were far more street-wise. Now began what is my recognition of the many accents and characteristics of the varied areas of our British Isles.

The others were from South Wales, the valleys and Cardiff or they were Brummies. They were capable of dealing with this new environment and to recognize and exploit any relaxation shown by the N.C.O's in charge. We two bucolics were strangers in their midst and became the butt of many jokes and ill-deserved attention.

Serious questions like, "Where's Gloucestershire?" were more easily explained by saying, "It's to the west of Oxfordshire", and most could then relate.

Our first visit to the parade ground, where the sergeant showed up, soon sorted out those who, "Don't know their left from their right", and those who had failed to learn their new army number. Every member of H.M. forces is allotted their own, which they will learn and remember for the rest of their lives. One test of the validity of the claims of the acquaintances in later life, is to ask them their army number. There should be an instant and fast rendition, even though fifty years or more have passed.

"Right, fall in, in two lines and when I reach you, you will shout out your name and the last three", (the last three numbers of your army number). My number being 14825749 meant me always answering, when challenged, "Lazenby 749, Sir."

The infamous term "Square Bashing" became a painful reality.

"This afternoon, you are all going to the cinema."

We did. Having been told that we were all "confined to camp" for the first week, we were then confronted by the dreadful realities of Venereal Disease. Slides projected on the screen, displayed the results of advanced syphilis, gonorrhoea etcetera. Enough to keep many of we virgin soldiers from any thought of contact with the fairer sex.

Any man who was hospitalised and unable to perform their army duties would find that cash allowances to family or wives would automatically cease. This would be a dead giveaway and bring into question the poor chap's morals.

"Next week you will be allowed out and will probably visit the 'Welcome Club' in Worcester.

We know there are women there from whom you could catch VD so be warned."

The whole thing sounded so revolting that, in my case, for one, my virginity continued for some time. Yes, years later, the book, "The Virgin Soldiers", by Leslie Thomas, recalled many memories. In the 1940's there were still plenty around. I guess the same could hardly be said for today's youth.

And yes, the image of an instrument pushed right up the penis, which then released a metal, miniature umbrella-shape allowing puss to be scraped out on its withdrawal, was enough to make your eyes water!

On later occasions, visiting the 'Welcome Club' caused apprehension and a reluctance to enjoy the most innocent of approaches by the genuine and good ladies, who were doing their best to feed and entertain these newly conscripted lads.

"Cor, look at those blokes", said the chap next to me, on a march outside the confines of our own parade ground.

"Those blokes" were more squaddies who'd finished the initial six weeks basic training and had been assigned to one or the other of the Worcester or South Staffs regiments. They were now infantry men and if my squad thought that life was harsh, the sight of them being toughened up, hurling great logs of timber around, made the heart sink.

"I don't want to do that", I thought and made a very conscious decision to make every effort to avoid it. Had we already been told that we, drawn from the garage trade, were destined for the R.E.M.E. (Royal Electrical and Mechanical Engineers) and that every soldier, no matter what happened afterwards, would get this punishing, six weeks Basic Training, we would have had a very different perspective on life. This lack of knowledge led me to present quite the wrong impression to our mentors who would have been told to assess each individual's potential.

Over these long weeks, we learnt that "the Army is always right". Only once was I put on "Jankers". This word covered many unpleasant tasks, from cleaning the loos to peeling spuds etc. My task was to scrub the gym floor with a nailbrush.

We were issued with rifles that we had to clean and clean, for which purpose the squaddies kit contained a pull through, wadding and oil; they were Lee-Enfield, 303's, unchanged from the ones used in World War 1, heavy but sturdy.

Then came a visit to the rifle range. I'd always been a good rifleman with the smaller 2.2, but being left-handed, I was awkward amongst the others, having to reach over the barrel after every shot, to pull back the bolt which ejected the spent casing and then slam it back after the next bullet had pushed up from the magazine. Suddenly realising that I was doing very well, I imagined being selected for an infantry sniper and deliberately messed up.

Another day we were introduced to observation tests. After much talk about middle distance and background, we were asked to find some camouflaged targets in front of us, where we were standing on high ground. They were all totally obvious to me, but fearing again that good eyesight might be useful to the infantry, I assured Lance Corporal Hoseason that I couldn't see them properly and backed this up by explaining I'd been rejected by the R.A.F. for colour blindness. Not very convincing, less so since I recently discovered that those of us so afflicted, are in fact, better at distinguishing such objects.

This Lance Corporal Hoseason was the most objectionable young man that it has ever been my bad luck to encounter. Other than physical brutality he employed every possible means of getting at me. With the rifle in hand I toyed seriously with the idea of shooting him. Conceivably this could be done while we were all standing in line practising with blank ammunition. My devilish scheme was, when home for a weekend break, to take back a live bullet from my father's desk and to sneak it amongst the others. Patently I dropped the idea, for otherwise I wouldn't be writing this, but would have been "shot at dawn". The name Hoseason has been etched in my memory, and when I hired a boat to chug around the Norfolk Broads, I made damn sure that it didn't belong to those Broads specialists, the Hoseason company!

Towards the end of this dreadful experience we were given a simple trade test. This involved assembling an adjustable spanner, some filing and some measuring etc, as well as linking together a lavatory pull chain. The chain stayed unassembled. Soon after, we were interviewed by the officer in charge and told our destiny. We were to be posted to London where the R.E.M.E. had workshops in Catford. What a relief, even though I was dismayed that all the other intake was coming too. A number of them had taken their cue from our instructors and indulged themselves in bullying the country lads. I'd have enjoyed reflecting on their fate if they had been left behind for infantry training.

A weekend pass was given and I went home by train to Shipton Station, where my father was waiting. I felt good, both physically and mentally. This was the point at which we adolescent youths began a very quick metamorphosis into adulthood. Were it only possible for today's younger generation to be so actively inspired and disciplined, the country would be a far better place to live in.

Now began a different understanding between father and son. The man who had kept me all those years in submission – so bad, that at the age of 10 years old, my mother was advised to get me away for a couple of weeks – I had even started stuttering because of my nerves – began to become human.

Throwing caution to the wind – remember, he was restricted to a ten mile radius – he drove me back to barracks in fine style.

After a final passing-out parade – which really looked and felt quite good, we screamed our goodbyes to that dreadful period and were entrained to London. This was the last time I'd see Lea and Perrins Worcestershire sauce factory alongside the railway lines, but made a mental note to try some when it became available.

At this point, I made a conscious decision to present a much harder face to the world; it did work. Long after, when I'd been in Egypt for a while, one of my tormentors, who had just arrived, all white and pasty, remarked just how much I had changed!

Arriving at Paddington, we were hustled, in full kit, rifles to hand, into more army trucks. We crossed the Thames, the first time for me, and were deposited at a bomb-blasted house in Lewisham, on a rising bit of ground. This was to be our home for the next three weeks. The windows were all blown out and the rooms quite empty except for the paliasses on the bare boards.

Nonetheless, there was a lot of excitement in the air. This was soon tempered by the realization that those funny engine noises, which suddenly stopped and were followed by a loud explosion, were made by "doodlebugs". These were the German V 1's and we appeared to be in "bomb alley". During our time there we actually watched some of them approach and said little private prayers to ourselves that their engines would continue buzzing – buzz bombs was another popular name for them – until they were past us. They did, all but one, until over a bit to the west, it was seen to dive down causing the now familiar explosion not very far away.

Over the next three weeks, we had to rise and make our way down to Catford R.E.M.E. workshops. Our transport was the faithful old London tram. The journey took us past Lewisham Obelisk, sited in the centre of a busy road junction. At Catford we found the regimental discipline utterly relaxed. Our time was spent in classrooms and workshops. Other diversions were available. Visits to the Victorian Public Baths – a first for me – to the cinema and the theatre where Max Miller "the cheeky chappy" was playing. A good many pints of London ales were tested.

At the end of this course came individual postings. In this, I had perhaps been too clever. By far the majority were sent to Arborfield near Reading for six months training in mechanical engineering, something from which I would surely have benefited. Oh no, I'd done too well in the tests and was posted to Bicester Garrison. This eventually served me well being only thirty miles from home.

Bicester was the hub for massive army commitments. It had its own railway system serving the R.A.O.C. (Royal Army Ordinance Corps) at Graven Hill and Ambroseden, a formidable A.T.S. camp at Piddington and much more. I was assigned to the R.E.M.E. camp at Arncott and billeted in one of B company's Nissan huts, which held some sixteen "craftsmen".

I was to work in 21 Workshop, one of several huge repair buildings right next to the camp. The clothing was denims, a blouse top and trousers serving as overalls. We new arrivals experienced a bit of resentment. It appears we were drafted in to replace a contingent of squaddies who had upset the routine by staging a mutiny of some kind. They had been quickly split up and posted overseas. Little did I suspect that I'd become a mutineer, a long way in the future.

I was to stay at Arncot for about eighteen months. The day started when the company bugler, who bunked along with us, blew reveille at 6a.m. You'd know when he had had a rough night because it was then far from perfect. It was with some amusement that he might be seen, hut door propped open by one foot, far enough for the bugle to protrude, while he at the same time, relieved himself in a great steaming arc onto the path outside.

After breakfast, it was in a very disorderly column that we marched down to the workshop. Ours was a vast structure with travelling overhead cranes to each of the four long bays. The crane drivers were perched "up in the Gods" all day long except when nature called, which was always just when you needed them. It was a tank repair workshop undertaking complete overhauls of Churchills and Shermans.

For a brief spell I was on the Shermans. Their radial engines consisted of five, 6 cylinder Chrysler engine blocks bolted to one common casing. These petrol driven tanks later switched to diesel engines. The petrol model had been particularly vulnerable under attack and ignited so easily. To get to this engine it was necessary to remove an extremely heavy armoured plate from underneath. All the waste oil and other gunge collected on it would empty over the unwary fitter.

But quite soon two bays were cleared out and a constant flow of Willys and Ford Jeeps were brought in. They were to be completely stripped and rebuilt. We craftsmen were paired off to work as teams. My colleague was Allun Jones; need I say that he was Welsh and the son of a typical Welsh mining family from Ogmore Vale. He was short, squat and immensely strong. We both had similar work experience, both from small, rural garages, used to working hard and able to tackle any light vehicle repairs. The Jeeps were stripped of body and all mechanical parts. Engines, gear-boxes, axles etc being sent to other departments for overhaul.

The Jeep is a very sensible and conveniently, a simple vehicle. The engine could be removed by two men in a matter of minutes; just a few key bolts had the body off, and so on. The rebuild was just as simple. Because both Ford and Willys were made to exactly the same specification, except for one front chassis member, the rebuilt vehicle would be a mixture of both makes. The present day "purist restorers" of these amazing relics, get quite upset when they find they've been sold a "hotch potch". They want every bolt, let alone major components, to match exactly.

The Ford bolts were all produced with the letter F moulded on the head. These people relieve their frustration by moaning and blaming my colleagues and me. Our working week included all day Saturday and Sunday morning.

To prepare one batch of Jeeps for air-borne drops, we had to reduce weight and dimensions by shortening the front bumper, fitting a fast release nut to allow the steering wheel's removal and discard other bits. Then, there we were, Taffy and me slogging our hearts out for the war effort, when the unthinkable happened. We were called aside by some "hard boys" and told to ease up because "You're carving the job up." My first and only clash with unionism.

I was lucky, with Bicester being near enough, to get home frequently. This required a journey to Bicester station on the Garrison train; another train ride to Oxford and a bus ride to Burford. The train ran to the old Midland railway station. My cousin, Mary, worked the evening shift in the ticket office, which was sited in the middle of the large, covered concourse. Very few squaddies bought tickets and managed to avoid the collector at Bicester by getting out of the wrong side of the coach onto the rail line and walking out unobserved.

One event which still makes me cringe, is the time I got out at Arncot and, to avoid waiting for the train to move on, crossed in front of it. All was dark except for a small light on the front of the engine and I trapped my foot under the rail. I couldn't immediately remove it until seconds before the train moved forward. That brief time seemed like an eternity! The Lord must have been watching, no one else could! I never repeated that stupid idea.

After some months, petrol rationing was relaxed and a few monthly coupons were granted to private car owners. Suddenly, comparative freedom was possible. My father owned a 1937 Morris 8, two-seater tourer. This had been on hire to R.A.F. Little Rissington and was used, with a W.A.A.F. driver, to carry an officer around the airfield. It had been "decommissioned", returned to father and was standing on blocks in the barn. He gave it to me and I became one of a very small, privileged number of car owners on camp.

This car became a very popular transport for army mates and a great attraction for the opposite sex. Drunken pub-crawls to Thame, Islip and other villages were common. My previous experience of packing them in allowed me, hood down, to fit five of us in. Several skirmishes with A.T.S. girls ensued; all innocent, by today's standards. Then I began a long lasting attachment with a lovely Bicester girl. She was Michelle Hart, a blonde, with a French mother and quite wonderful.

The car also meant that I could go home for short visits. All my childhood I'd had to be a very regular churchgoer, my grandfather being the organist and choirmaster. This had lapsed, until I found that if I went on Church Parade every Sunday morning, I was excused from workshop duty. This meant that after the 11 a.m. service, not well attended by others, I was able to drive home, already dressed in my best uniform.

Weekend passes became more frequent. The company C.O. also ran a car and it was to our mutual advantage that I would supply him with petrol coupons from my father's plentiful supply, in exchange for passes and soap coupons.

During the frequent times that I was at home, I helped my father with garage duties in the daytime. Nights were devoted to other pursuits. These consisted of endless pub-crawls, always with chasing ladies, being the main purpose.

Again, my car was a magnet and it worked very hard and well. Most of my friends were serving elsewhere in the forces. This meant that my usual companion was Mervyn Garratt. He was exempt from call-up because of his work at the R.A.F. Maintenance Unit. Many pints of beer were consumed, the popular pubs being The Crown at Langford and The Lamb at Filkins. The Crown has now been "developed" as private housing, and so too, I believe, has The Lamb.

Both villages were blessed with village halls, both having regular dances. Filkins was doubly blessed, both with attractive girls and a Womens' Land Army hostel. The dances, though well attended, were one-sided affairs. Few of us youths could dance, by which I mean ball-room dancing, and the odd hokey-cokey, – with the result that we sat around ogling this wonderful display. The girls had to pair up amongst themselves. One fancy-dress night springs to mind; Jean Trinder, the blacksmith's striking, blonde daughter, was wearing a grass skirt, and though too drunk to remember, I was told that I'd tried to set fire to it under the forbidding eye of her mother. Many mothers chaperoned their daughters, sitting on the side-lines and watching. Jean and Jean Truman, the watch and clock repairer's daughter, enjoyed many drives around the countryside in the faithful Morris car.

The Land Girls favoured The Crown at Langford. It was by no means a large pub, but became crammed out every night. Local lads buzzed round it like bees round a honey-pot. Mervyn, a natural and good pianist, was always welcome and played an endless medley of popular songs, "Roll out the barrel" and "She'll be coming round the mountain" for instance. This became the inevitable singsong in which every drunken voice took part. Not content with buying him more beer than he could drink, a reveller flipped open the top of the long-suffering piano and poured beer down into the works on more than one occasion, "Give her a drink Merv". He was taken to task by Mr. Catchpole, the landlord for trying to seduce his fifteen-year-old daughter, Pat, but was allowed to keep coming, because of his musical talent.

The Land Army hostel was the country house of the politician, Sir Stafford Cripps. The warden, Mrs. Boyd, was liked by all, even though the rules set down were inflexible and the girls were required to be back inside by 10p.m. Some five minutes before that deadline, she would come out on to the front steps and ring a hand bell, shouting loudly, "Come along girls, it's time you were in". As if by magic, her charges would appear from various areas. Car doors slammed and bushes shook as they discharged their young lovers and then the door was bolted. Latecomers, usually the same girls each time, attracted the attention of their friends inside and clambered through an opened window. The deadline wasn't really too harsh as the pub closed at 10p.m. There were always girls who wanted a ride back to the hostel, sometimes with a useful margin of time to spare! Consequently, there would be time for a "snogging session" and some adolescent fumbling and exploration of the young lady. Because of my age, eighteen plus, most of the girls were a few years older and perhaps more experienced.

I was once subjected to the worst put-down of my life. My lady of that night suddenly shouted to her friend, who was with Mervyn, in a similar predicament, "Ay oop Lizzie, ees bluedy passion's rising" in a loud, mocking Yorkshire accent. A lasting joke for Mervyn and me for the rest of our days.

The Crown got so packed with bodies that it was near impossible to find a way back to the doorway, once well inside. Those needing a quick exit for a "call of nature" would climb through the window. Whilst the men had the advantage of a very crude outside loo, the girls had nowhere and had to climb amongst the nearby bushes. The villagers also used the pub. One small, elderly man heralded his advance by intoning, "Make way for a naval officer", in a reedy, querulous voice and was followed by his equally diminutive wife, who scolded him for any breach of proper conduct.

There were also two, pretty, blonde, local girls. I was pleasantly surprised on my return home from overseas service, to find that Keith Herbert, who had been born in the house next to mine, had married one of them. Now he and Jenny live in that same house.

Came the day, that to mark V.E. day – Victory in Europe – our Bicester garrison was called on to march through Oxford. Much time was devoted to smartening up on our parade ground.

"Come on, put some swank into it" was the order of the day.

"Straighten up and look as though you are enjoying it" And to tell the truth, it was enjoyable as we marched through Oxford "swanking it" with pride.

All this time, my steady girlfriend, Mimi, and I spent many pleasant evenings touring the Bicester area and its varied inns. The Red Cow at Chesterton was a favourite.

Alas, this whole cosy existence was about to end.

In February 1946, I was on a short leave at home. On coming home for lunch, my mother gave me some devastating news. My company commander, the Captain, of petrol coupon swap fame, had telephoned her. The message was that I could extend my leave in preparation for an overseas posting. This unusual, personal touch was probably prompted by his realization that his petrol supply was about to be decimated.

"I've done all I could to prevent this", he said, "but I'm afraid he'll have to go, I'm sorry."

Well, at least the war in Europe was over and few dangers were anticipated.

On return to camp I was sent with full kit to Otley Moor, Yorkshire. It was a holding camp where troops were assembled, previous to embarking. The weather was cold and bleak and we were housed in the usual Nissan huts with just the "tortoise" stove, glowing red in the centre.

Here, my first attempt at laundry was to wash my socks in the icy cold water, which was all that we had for our ablutions, and put them near the stove to dry. It was with some concern that, when I came to wear them they had shrunk to about half the size.

We were allowed into Otley in the evenings and consumed huge quantities of Yorkshire beer. Once we went on to the local cinema but got chucked out for being so noisy. I was still learning about life.

One evening, while several of us were gathered around a large wooden table in a pub, I found myself sitting next to an unsavoury looking woman who was years older than myself. Soon, a whispered advice from a local at the far end of the bar, was passed round to me,

"Don't have anything to do with that one. She'll give you a dose up."

Never had there been any chance.

Weaving back in an alcoholic daze, three of us were crossing the bridge over the River Wharfe way down below, when my left hand companion decided he'd jump over the parapet. I managed to restrain him, but have often mulled over its probable result had I also have been incapable.

We had to attend a kit parade and were issued with light khaki drill. Shirts, shorts and even some socks with no feet in them. This was purely for effect to show above gaiters. A new "blanco" was ominous, it being white and all belts, gaiters and webbing equipment would have to change colour from its present, dull, orange.

Thankfully, our stay on that cold moor was quite short. Orders were issued to pack up and we were taken by rail to Newhaven. A number of the young squaddies had never seen the sea, let alone the English Channel. The train took us right down to the docks where we were transferred to a transport ship and headed out for Dieppe. Arriving there, having been surrounded by sea-sick personnel – I was always a good sailor and never smitten with that problem – the evidence of war was only too apparent.

In their wisdom, it had been decided by the war lords to make a trial run and that a major assault should be made on the port, long before the D-Day invasion; predominately Canadian troops were employed. They suffered very severe losses. Shelling had decimated the harbour area and many of the waterfront buildings were only ruined shells. Little had yet been done to repair the damage.

Our money was now converted into French francs. The rate had been 480 to the pound but only a couple of weeks before it was doubled to 960! Another stroke of luck.

Our accommodation was a real revelation to us. We were billeted in some ex German army huts. But what huts they were, large and airy, generous windows and built of timber. Situated on top of the cliffs behind the port, they also afforded a panoramic view of the sea. It would have been great to stay there. At night, the group from our hut made a sortie down into the town. An unfamiliar corporal assumed charge of this venture. He was somewhat older than the rest and soon got us into a harbour side bar. The "bier" and the wine flowed and he led us in singing the most crude and dreadful songs that I have ever heard. Naturally, we all joined in.

A rendition of "There were three Jews from Jerusalem" with shocking chorus lines, went down with the locals, who, with hand clapping and appreciative laughter, enthusiastically sang along.

My embarrassment was only saved by the realization that they'd no idea what they were attempting to sing, I hope.

Too soon we were entrained for an overnight journey to Toulon. The railway coaches were typical compartments. Seats either side with net luggage racks above, six of us to each. Lots were drawn for sleeping positions, one to each long seat, one to each luggage rack and one to each space under the seats. I opted for the luggage rack, deciding that I'd rather be the one to fall on the fellow below than be crushed should the luggage rack occupant fall out. The French railways were yet to be modernised to today's formidable efficiency and it was a long journey before we reached the Mediterranean.

At Toulon we changed our transport to a small convoy of British Army trucks. After a short drive along a wonderful coast road, sun shining on palm trees and by now, pleasantly warm, we were disgorged in a tented camp at Hyeres. Contrast that with Ottley Moor! The French pronunciation for this town confounded many, who persisted in calling it High-ers.

Inevitably, we wished to explore this little town. Talk of French brothels had been rife and a group of us set out to seek their existence. We managed to convey to a small boy that we were looking for some "jig-a-jig". After being bribed with a packet of fags, (which were the preferred currency), he led us through quaint streets, where from laundry-festooned balconies, we were scrutinised by a host of old crones, dressed in black with lacy, black head-scarves. Our guide shouted our mission and they cat-called, jeered and cackled with laughter. It has since bothered me that the cigarette packet given to the lad had been doctored. The cigarettes had been cut in half and the bottom of the pack stuffed with paper. The other halves would receive the same treatment in an empty pack.

We arrived at an open square and a building, with a heavy, iron-studded door and a metal grille where a window should be, was pointed out. After a few tentative knocks, a shutter was slid aside and a face showed in the gloom. After deciding that we were business the door was opened to us. The disbelief and unease of the young squaddies was palpable, a real brothel!

The interior was dark after the Mediterranean sun. Steps leading down to the basement were guarded by Madam, who required admission money. There was a crude bar for drinks, at inflated prices, several trestle tables and chairs with a huddle of soldiers sitting around them and a flight of stairs leading up to a surrounding balcony, from which several doors led off. These doors would regularly open and disgorge a khaki clad soldier, followed by the lady who had just satisfied his demands. The whole atmosphere was incredibly sad and seedy. These others were very brown, sunburnt "old soldiers". They were some of the, soon to be demobbed, campaign men in transit from the Middle and Far East, who hadn't been home for years. This could well have been their first chance to enjoy a woman since arriving in India or Burma years before. No time to be pickish or squeamish! None of our pale, youthful group seemed likely to experiment.

A door opened, and, after a language problem, we realised we were invited to pay to go through to witness an "Exibish". None wishing to "chicken out", we parted with more francs and were admitted to another large room, which had rows of seats around a central space. We were soon seated and watching a couple of uninviting ladies performing a series of extremely tortuous acts, made possible by the use of a huge penis strapped on one of them. This was obviously to get their audience "fired up". For me, and, as I later discovered, most of the others, it was terribly off-putting. The red burn marks on their pathetic shanks were soon explained, when, at critical moments, one or other of the "old soldiers" hopped up from their seats and stubbed their cigarette butts on the writhing flesh, to cause even more exertion.

"Exibish" over, we repaired to the drinking den, only to be appalled at seeing these same two women escorting some of their audience to the nether regions, up the stairs. This entertainment soon jaded and we left intact, with much relief.

That was Hyeres and the next day it was back to Toulon where we boarded a troop carrier. We were dispersed to its several decks, allocated a hammock, told where the "heads" (loos) were and where the mess deck could be found. Back on the upper deck we could see all the harbour, passage through which was very restricted by a number of French warships, which had been deliberately scuttled to avoid capture by the Nazis when France capitulated. Their superstructures, masts and some rigging were still above the water level and disclosed their location. Why didn't they sail to join our Allied Forces?

Up with the anchor on its heavy, rattling chain and out onto an unbelievably blue Mediterranean. No sooner were we on our way than,

"Right you lot, name and last three."

A little runt of a Catering Corps sergeant materialized from nowhere at the bottom of a companion-way, where a group of us were about to go back up on deck.

"You'll report to the cooks for mess deck duties."

Employing some cunning, I clapped my hand to my mouth, looked desperate and managed to convey that I was about to be seasick.

"Move out of the way and let this man through" was the welcome result. I shot up those steps really fast and breathed sighs of relief that I'd escaped that dreary fate.

A Mediterranean cruise is commonplace these days, but not then. The contrast to cold and dismal Britain could hardly have been more marked. The usual boat drill had to be taken seriously, since mines were floating around in many areas. Wonderful sights of Stromboli, the Straits of Bonifacio, followed later by views of Etna while going through the Straits of Messina, were nothing short of magical.

Yes, one day I did find myself peeling great quantities of spuds, while sitting right up in the bows watching porpoises frolicking around. And what food we were served! Long forgotten delicacies, like white bread instead of the grey stuff, which had been our staple diet since the war began. Oranges, which had been non-existent at home for years, real eggs, instead of that tasteless reconstituted egg powder, and lashings of beef.

CHAPTER FIVE

Egypt

This idyll had to end and it did when we first saw a finger of low-lying land which heralded our arrival to the north end of the Suez Canal; it was dominated by a statue to deLeseppes, the brain behind this momentous achievement. We stood off Port Said long enough to marvel at the "bum boats" which came out to meet us. Their owners, clad in long, dirty, white galabiyahs, threw lines to some interested customers and the bartering began. We'd already changed our English money for Egyptian piastres, dubbed "ackers", one hundred to the pound. They were probably the only new notes we would ever see, those in general circulation being incredibly dog-eared and scruffy. Business was mainly by sign language and deals were struck in a mixture of broken English and a counting of fingers. Baskets were loaded in the boats, hauled up, and money returned by the same route. Rather incongruously, a couple of the traders were red-heads, a testimony to the pioneering Jocks in the years gone by.

We soon came alongside and disembarked. Egypt astonished us immediately. The smells of the port and its denizens invaded us. The natives were in various garbs but most in their long galabiyahs. Our preparation for all these strange sights and smells was written in an army booklet

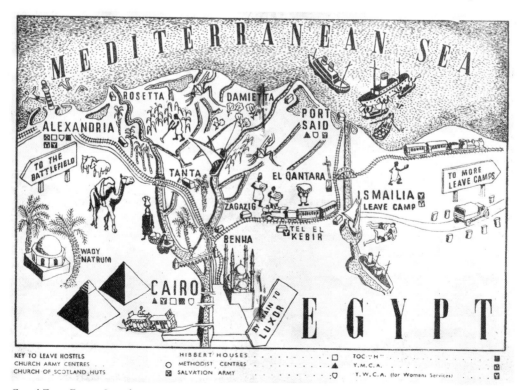

Canal Zone Forces Introductory map

Safety First

– "Middle East Theatre" with a foreword signed by the Commander-in-Chief, Middle East Forces. I still have mine to hand and so that you may be able to understand the attitudes of the day, I feel able to quote verbatim some of its contents, now and later on:

INTRODUCTION

You may have a variety of ideas of the Middle East when you get off the boat. If you're feeling a little worse for wear, it may strike you as a disorderly pattern of garish light, raucous noises and pungent smells, with far too much sun and sand, and too many flies and people. If you're romantically disposed on the other hand, you may think of it as the scene of dusty, desert battles or of starry, blue nights and silhouetted minarets of Cleopatra or Richard Coeur de Lion.

It all has its place in the complete picture of course, but if the Middle East is to be something more than just another overseas station, coloured with romantic or distasteful associations, you'll want to know something about the geographical and historical facts that made this corner of the Mediterranean one of the most important and interesting places on the earth's surface. And in any case you will want to know how not to get yourself robbed or swindled, or become sick and bored.

THE EVERYDAY SCENE

Egypt is a country vital to Britain's trade routes. What will you see around you there? You will see the Egyptian peasant, or fellah. He is overworked, almost as poor as it's possible to be, diseased, gay, and dimly conscious of the long past in his superstitions. The fellahin women, in their black draperies, ride into the cities squatting in swarms on donkey carts; they are often veiled and can carry loads on their heads with remarkable skill. Modern irrigation has increased the area of land under cultivation along the river and the population has increased, almost beyond the capacity of the land to support it. Labour is, thus, very cheap, both on the land and in the cities of Cairo and Alexandria, which are crowded with cleaners and carriers, shoe-shines and pedlars of every kind of goods. There are lots of beggars who ask for baksheesh. Many of those who accost you are potential thieves. Do not attempt to stay in any place that is not in bounds or you will probably be robbed. Always look for the recognised price list in a hotel, café or bar. The native will never undercharge you.

These are only samples of the introduction to the new arrivals. Little wonder that the squaddies' attitudes to the natives were more than a little biased against them.

Now came the last part of our journey, by rail, heading south from Port Said. Apart from the obvious changes, the sand, the dust and the heat, there were other distractions. The lush strips of cultivated land irrigated by the freshwater canals fed from the Nile, the amusing sight of black-clad women, struggling to keep up with their men who were riding donkeys at a fast jog-trot and the less amusing sight of a notice board which read, "You are now entering a Malarial Area."

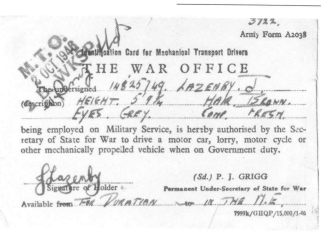

Journey's end was the massive army depot of Tel-el-Kebir, with its twenty seven mile perimeter fence. The check point barrier was raised and we were debussed from the trucks which had met us at the station; on to a parade ground surrounded by wooden army huts. I was sent to Hut 23. It was nice and airy with rows of beds down either side and the usual room for the corporal and lance-corporal.

The iron beds with slatted, metal bases, each having its own locker and shelf space, seemed inviting in the semi-dark, window shutters keeping the sun out. Next, an issue of mosquito nets, blankets and overalls. The other hut inmates soon came back from their workshops, most working in No.117.

The N.A.A.F.I.-E.F.I. (Expeditionary Forces Institutes), was close by, and, after an evening meal, some refreshment was called for. The beer was served in extraordinary glasses. These were empty beer bottles that had been filled to a preset level with hot water and then plunged into icy

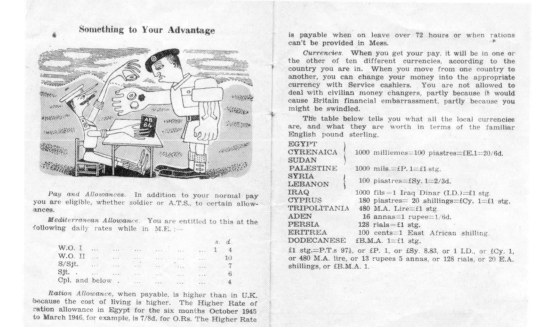

Something to Your Advantage

Pay and Allowances. In addition to your normal pay you are eligible, whether soldier or A.T.S., to certain allowances.

Mediterranean Allowance. You are entitled to this at the following daily rates while in M.E.:—

	s.	d.
W.O. I	1	4
W.O. II		10
S/Sjt.		7
Sjt.		6
Cpl. and below		4

Ration Allowance, when payable, is higher than in U.K. because the cost of living is higher. The Higher Rate of ration allowance in Egypt for the six months October 1945 to March 1946, for example, is 7/8d. for O.Rs. The Higher Rate

32

is payable when on leave over 72 hours or when rations can't be provided in Mess.

Currencies. When you get your pay, it will be in one or the other of ten different currencies, according to the country you are in. When you move from one country to another, you can change your money into the appropriate currency with Service cashiers. You are not allowed to deal with civilian money changers, partly because it would cause Britain financial embarrassment, partly because you might be swindled.

The table below tells you what all the local currencies are, and what they are worth in terms of the familiar English pound sterling.

EGYPT	
CYRENAICA	} 1000 milliemes=100 piastres=£E.1=20/6d.
SUDAN	
PALESTINE	1000 mils.=£P. 1=£1 stg.
SYRIA	} 100 piastres=£Sy. 1=2/3d.
LEBANON	
IRAQ	1000 fils=1 Iraq Dinar (I.D.)=£1 stg.
CYPRUS	180 piastres= 20 shillings=£Cy. 1=£1 stg.
TRIPOLITANIA	480 M.A. Lire=£1 stg.
ADEN	16 annas=1 rupee=1/6d.
PERSIA	128 rials=£1 stg.
ERITREA	100 cents=1 East African shilling.
DODECANESE	£B.M.A. 1=£1 stg.

£1 stg.=P.T.s 97½, or £P. 1, or £Sy. 8.83, or 1 I.D., or £Cy. 1, or 480 M.A. lire, or 13 rupees 5 annas, or 128 rials, or 20 E.A. shillings, or £B.M.A. 1.

33

Something to Write Home About

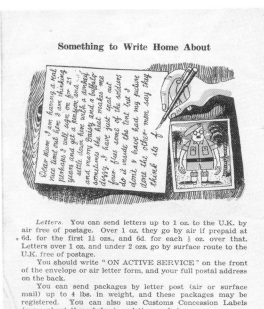

Letters. You can send letters up to 1 oz. to the U.K. by air free of postage. Over 1 oz. they go by air if prepaid at 6d. for the first 1½ ozs., and 6d. for each ½ oz. over that. Letters over 1 oz. and under 2 ozs. go by surface route to the U.K. free of postage.

You should write " ON ACTIVE SERVICE " on the front of the envelope or air letter form, and your full postal address on the back.

You can send packages by letter post (air or surface mail) up to 4 lbs. in weight, and these packages may be registered. You can also use Customs Concession Labels (more about these below) on letter packets.

Parcels. You can send two gift parcels per month (including Customs Concession parcels) to the same person in the U.K. The parcels mustn't exceed 11 lbs. each in total weight, of which up to 7 lbs. may be foodstuffs. No foodstuff (apart from fruit) may be exported from Palestine.

Parcels are normally subject to duty and purchase tax on arrival in U.K., but parcels bearing a Customs Concession Label are exempt. You can send 24 of these a year up to a total value of £12. You can obtain these labels from your unit (they call them A.F. W5192's in the Orderly Room) to cover values from 10/- to £12, in 10/- stages. Customs concession parcels mustn't contain:

Drinkable spirits.

More than ½ lb. of tobacco (200 cigarettes or 50 cigars).

Tobacco and cigarettes marked " H.M. Ships only " or " N.A.A.F.I. Supplies for the Forces."

More than ½ pint (10 fluid ozs.) of perfume.

More than 2 lbs. of any one foodstuff.

Any article purchased from Naval or E.F.I./N.A.A.F.I. Canteens if imported from U.K. or North America.

Any article whose export from M.E. or transmission by post is forbidden by General or Command Orders.

The only fresh fruits you may send are grapefruit, oranges, lemons and limes. Send the unripe fruit. Wrap it carefully and pack in wicker baskets or stout wooden boxes with ventilation holes. Mark the parcel " Fruit only."

If you wish to send home articles for your personal use on return to U.K., these can go by parcel post up to a limit of 22 lbs. Parcels should be clearly marked " Personal Effects," and mustn't contain gifts or articles for sale.

Every parcel must contain a slip giving the name and address of the sender and the person to whom the parcel is being sent. Parcels (as distinct from letter packets) can't be sent by registered post.

Postage rates for parcels to U.K. are:—

Not exceeding	3 lbs. in weight	—	9d.
"	"	7 " " "	— 1/6
"	"	11 " " "	— 2/-
"	"	22 " " "	— 3/6

34

35

water causing them to fracture just below the neck. Although attempts were made to smooth the sharp edges, some were quite lethal.

I was soon introduced to the workshops, the lieutenant in charge and the motley crew of local Egyptians who would be doing all the dirty, heavy work. It was a B vehicle – not armoured-repair and overhaul unit. The most common vehicles were A.E.C. Matadors, Diamond T. tank transporters and Scammel recovery vehicles, all equipped with powerful winches.

Army discipline was very relaxed. The only bull-shit parade was for overnight guard duty, which was followed by a day off. There was always an extra name on the roster to provide against the absence of a guard through illness. As usual the best turned out guard was told to fall out and be excused duty. I never achieved that standard. The various patrol duties were distributed and a night of vigilance was called for. In fact, most retired to their bunks and laid down until time to regroup and fall out. There were times when a hasty retreat through the back door was called for but it was likely that the guard commanders themselves were skiving off. No one was ever charged for dereliction of duty.

There were two types of latrines. One consisted of long boards to sit on, with buckets below, which were emptied daily by a fellah. Though out in the open they were particularly smelly and putrid in the scorching summer heat. A good breeding area for the tiny mites which attacked the scrotum area, resulting in a case of "the crabs". This meant a report to the M.O. who gave orders to shave off, so that a white liquid could be painted on the itchy bits.

The other latrines were of cunning construction. A circular wall of mud bricks was laid. Labourers then dug out the sand in the middle and that from under the wall. This then dropped down and another course of bricks was cemented on. This progressed until a hole some fifteen feet was achieved. On cross beams, a floor was laid and a circle of independent seats arranged in the centre. The whole was then roofed over.

For night-time use a five gallon drum with the top cut out and fitted with a wire handle was left outside each hut and emptied each morning by one of the "Shite wallahs". The Egyptians were

Hut 23. Christmas 1946

perhaps more hygienic. They carried a tin can of water with them to wash themselves and often scraped a hole in the desert which they filled back in.

Most of my time was spent on the repair line with weekends free. Anything that was achieved was only due to the efforts of the native workers. We Askaris (army personnel) seemed only to carry out tasks of supervision, wandering down the line and calling on the workforce to shuggle (work) harder and not be so baltaggy (lazy). Each vehicle had a list of faults chalked on it – Arabic numbers and writing. A few of us troubled to learn to count to a hundred and recognize the numbers, but the written word was far too difficult. The only sentences in regular use were used to shout at the poor devils, calling their parentage into question, and dreadful cursing to urge them on, backed up with threatening gestures.

Winter weekends were for football, played on the hard, sand pitch in front of our hut. It was so hard that a tragic accident happened. A forward from one team was racing towards the opponents' goal, when, having pushed the ball a little too far, he was beaten by the goalie. It was such a hard tackle that he crashed down hitting his head with such impact that he was "knocked out" and never regained consciousness. He was a married man and left his widow with two children to support. A spontaneous collection was made and the resultant cash was sent to help her.

Most of my working time was spent on Matadors. When ready, we had to trial drive them, often in bare chassis form. At any useful speed we caused great dust clouds. To regularize things all ranks involved had to pass a driving test. This started with the question,

"Can you drive?"

Two drunken Jocks with overnight urinal at the ready

My bed and kit. Note pin ups

Me with footbal pitch in backgound

On assuring the sergeant that was the case, each was put into a small fifteen hundredweight Dodge and had to drive around a confined area. Although I had driven many thousands of miles, the "crash" gear box made me seem an amateur. It demanded a long pause between the necessary "double declutch" and grated horribly each time I used it. Sure that I must have failed miserably, it was, with some surprise, I found I'd passed. The production of this small document entitled me to drive any class of vehicle, there, or back in civvy street. Not bad for about a two minute test!

The company jeep, me, Bill Edmunds and Taffy Price

When I'd first arrived in Egypt the sudden heat caused splitting headaches for the first two weeks. I consumed aspirin at an alarming rate, one day taking fourteen. The blood needed to thin down in this highly charged youth! I have often wondered about its effect on many of those present day holiday-makers who spend just a few days in such climates. Consequently, I have always avoided such extremes. North Africa will not see me again.

Life took on a pattern as it usually will. Some days off were spent by arranging a trip to Cairo on the workshop liberty truck, an open-bodied 30 cwt. Dodge. This had crude seating on each side against the side boarding, giving a panoramic view of the many facets of this interesting land.

Doubtless the world and his wife go there now. I truly hope the place has changed since those days. It teemed with life and had an aroma of its own, not necessarily pleasant. The trams were so crowded with people hanging on their steps and door handles, even on the roofs, that I wonder that any fares were collected.

The Y.M.C.A. was a haven in all this turmoil, with its cool, pleasant gardens and big, airy rooms. Naturally, a trip out to Geiza and the pyramids was a must, though a sortie into the musty depths of the great pyramid of Cheops was probably not appreciated as it should have been. King Farouk had a palace close by.

In Cairo itself, instructions from some of the old hands had suggested "going up the Birka". This was an internationally known street of ill-repute, where "bints" were always available. The street was found, but looked far too unsavoury and hostile for further exploration.

Scammel recovery vehicle

117 Workshop

Diamond T's for repair

The Workshop run-about

Testing Matador Chassis

The use of the word "bint" was universal and referred to all ladies, even the ones at home. "I've got to write to my bint or she will finish with me" would have been quite normal talk.

Most of these forays descended into an alcoholic haze. Relations with the locals could hardly have been helped, when, leaving Cairo on the Canal Road, empty beer bottles were chucked into the path of following cars.

A week's leave was spent at Lake Timsah holiday camp near Ismalia; I have the flimsy brochure in front of me. A sample of its contents:

> Our sole object is to give you a thoroughly enjoyable holiday – do entirely as you please.
> Parades
> Nil – Anyone trying to parade will be examined by the M.O. or returned to his unit.

This was followed by lists of entertainments and leisure pursuits. There are always drawbacks to even the best of things and the following was only too necessary.

> Dress
> You may dress as you please within the camp, but you must wear trousers KD (Khaki Drill) and shirts with sleeves rolled down after 20.00 hours. Always sleep under your mosquito net, this is important in your own interest.

Believe me, the mosquitoes that breed so freely on Lake Timsah were there in vicious millions. Everyone suffered on their elbows, which inevitably rested against the "mozzy net".

Much time was spent lazing around and walking along to explore Ismailia. It is a pleasant enough town with wide, grassy banks and palm trees which run either side of the canal that runs through it, dubbed the "Sweet Water Canal". No name could be less true. After its passage through the arable land, which relied on it for irrigation, and for its manifold uses, bathing sweaty bodies, freshening up camels and oxen and its usefulness in disposing of putrefying bodies of dead animals and such like, it emptied into the Delta. Should any squaddie be unfortunate enough to fall, or be

American"White" Waggon

Getting down to it

Off to Cairo

*Me and Bill up the
Great Pyramid. Each stone
weighs 2¹/₂ tons*

thrown into it, he had to endure countless injections against countless infections.

Service personnel were segregated as usual: United Services Club (Officers only). Rendezvous and Blue Hive Clubs, (W.O's and Sergeants), Blue Kettle Club, Garden Club and Y.M.C.A (All other ranks). They were all quite pleasant but the Y.M.C.A. still conjures up a memory. Several of us stayed there for a weekend. Copious quantities of rum were quaffed and mine, with other ingested food and drink, was ejected out of the bedroom window. Rum has been anathema to me ever since. I'd never felt so ill before and the name and smell of it still haunts me.

British forces had been part of the local scene for generations and all mixed well together. I know that a few years after, when the Suez Crisis arose, things changed forever. The main prison, on one of the main streets, was only remarkable for its listless armed guards behind its iron railings and for the number of women, squatting in the dust against its walls, awaiting their incarcerated men-folk. It was the scene of a quite serious gunfight during the Suez Crisis.

Our only "enemies" were the hordes of shoe-shine boys who, on being rebuffed, would, given half a chance, chuck evil, liquid black polish over smart uniforms. One way of avoiding this dreaded action was to unbuckle the heavy army belt with its solid brass buckles and, swinging it around, threaten retaliation. There was also the undignified swift retreat, which looked a bit silly – a hefty squaddie running away from a diminutive shoe-shine wallah.

Back at T.E.K. we had our own "dhobi-wallahs". They were marvellous at washing and ironing all clothing. The ironing was done at tables out in the sun. With no such thing as steam irons, their very effective way of damping the ironing was to fill the mouth with water and spray it on in a controlled stream. At their regular calls to prayers they would be seen prostrating themselves on these same tables.

A sometime distraction would be to watch Egyptian vultures – shite hawks – who seemed happy to get caught in the frequent "dust devils" – miniature tornadoes – and be carried ever higher, trapped in its ascending funnel.

The time came when we were given two weeks leave. On offer were a Nile cruise to Luxor, a holiday camp in Nicosia (Cyprus) or a holiday camp in Alexandria. There was no contest! Legendary tales of the fleshpots of Sister Street in Alex decided, Bill Edmunds, Jock Crawford, Taffy Evans and me to test them out. In hindsight, Luxor would seem the obvious choice, but stone effigies of long-dead Kings and Queens held few attractions for red-blooded squaddies. Armed with all necessary documentation, leave passes, rail travel tickets, holiday bookings and brochures and reminders that any unguarded kit would go missing, we caught the train.

Egyptian trains, like their buses and trams, were always overflowing; many men, in their off-white galabiyahs, clinging on to all available outside projections, with others up on the roofs. The train joined the main Cairo to Alex line at Benha and went swiftly on to Tanta junction. On the way a strange thing happened – an arm shot through the open window, grabbed a kit bag from the overhead rack, and then the thief launched himself, with his loot, from the train which was going a "fair old lick". We saw him hit the ground and cartwheel away down the embankment. Also, as

Shoe shine boy

German P.O.W's guarding holiday camp

the train moved away from the platform at Tanta, another arm was thrust in and snatched the spectacles from the squaddie sitting opposite me. We all know that rather owl-like look which regular wearers make when they remove their glasses. Well, this chap's expression said it all, on top of needing to contemplate the next two weeks without them, he suffered a badly scratched nose from contact with a grubby fingernail.

Another valuable bit of advice was never ever to buy a bottle of mineral water or any foodstuffs offered on streets or station platforms. Their origins were of grave doubt – maybe the Sweet Water Canal – and would cause all sorts of gastro infections, known as "Gippy Tummy".

Our journey through the flat, fertile lands of the Nile Delta ended when we reported to the R.T.O. on the station platform at Alex. Transport was organised to our destination, "The Lone Palm Holiday Camp".

Here we settled in to "luxurious" hutted accommodation, the camp giving onto a blue and lazy Mediterranean. Many pastimes were available, but the urge to explore Alex was paramount. Next day, the delights of that city were sampled. Big department stores, full of goods, which had been impossible to find or buy back home, and teeming markets where we were pursued mercilessly by a colourful crowd of stall-holders. More shoe-shine boys, and then Sister Street.

Gateway to leave Camp Alexandria

CHAPTER SIX

Au Revoir Virginity

What an education! Both sides of the street were lined with bars and drinking dens. Some with tables outside where groups of men sat around smoking "hubble bubble" pipes.

The extraordinary first impression, was that of scenes from American cowboy films. This, because the bars were fitted with batwing doors, allowing glimpses into their dark interiors and the sight of female figures therein. Feeling like John Wayne we breasted the doors and ordered our drinks. Still that confounded Stella beer, but others too, on offer. Then came the ritual of pushing out of that bar, crossing the road and bursting into the next. After several such investigations, the journey between each getting more unsteady as the day progressed, a halt was called in the last one, so that some serious drinking and appraisal was called for.

There we were. Bill Edmunds, who became my bosom pal and with whom I still remain in contact, Jock Crawford, blonde little Taffy Evans and myself. Bill Edmunds is a typical Norfolk boy, dark and blessed with that lovely Norfolk accent ("Hey you got a light boy"?) which is particularly pronounced in those born in "The Marshes". His home, where I have been several times, was the little village of Brooke, off the Norwich to Bungay road. The house was, as most dwellings there, constructed from the local materials, mainly wood and wattle. So we were both country boys, talking the same language, even though mine is Gloucestershire.

We were quickly surrounded by dark-eyed bints, clamouring for us to buy them drinks, so they'd be allowed to stay and talk to us. This quickly became a rather expensive pastime, our own drinks seeming to be a fraction of the prices charged for the insipid looking concoctions the girls consumed with indecent haste.

The first day set the pattern for most of those to come, except that we became patrons of just that one establishment. In this way we formed a doubtful liaison with the same four girls. At each visit our familiarity advanced in direct relation to the depletion of our wallets.

"We're not buying them any more drinks until we get more than a promise of a bit of Jig-a-Jig they've talked about", declared Jock, who seemed eminently more experienced in sexual contact. And so it was agreed. Little Evans and I, both belated virgins, rather left the arrangements to him, while Edmunds just turned on his rather mischievous smile, which could mean just anything.

As a ploy we spent the next day at camp, to cause Sister Street some concern at our absence.

Our private beach lay next to a public one where both native families and white people were seen. Imagine our delight when one full-breasted, swim-clad girl wandered over. I see it now, this girl sitting and holding court while we lads sat, salivating, in a circle around her. We discovered that she was from a rather poor, French community, living a few hundred yards away. Naturally, a mild form of horseplay ensued, all of us striving to impress her with cartwheels, handstands and so on. Not to be outdone, this buxom wench took part, and to everyone's delight as she did a series of handstands, her melon-sized boobs conformed to gravity and popped up round her neck. This was too much for the lads who groaned with pent up passion. We were invited back to the family home. Soon the drink caused a call to nature; well, I've never seen a more filthy "small room" in my life and with hurried excuses I fled back to the camp! If people can live like that I really do not wish to know them.

Our next visit through the batwing doors evinced an enthusiastic welcome from "les girls". A serious discussion, over more drinks, concluded with a firm promise of action for the next day. I spent the next twenty-four hours in a state of eager, but uncertain anticipation. Was I, at last, about to join the ranks of those who'd "done it"?

At the arranged hour we arrived at the bar and, yes, our four girls were waiting. Whilst sinking the inevitable drink or two, the scheme was relayed to us. After suitable bartering an exorbitant price was fixed. Because they couldn't be seen walking with, or having any contact with us, we were instructed to follow a street length away. As they turned a corner at one end we were to have entered the other end. This seemed reasonable and so in a state of disbelief and agitation I, with the others, obeyed our orders and followed them. On turning a last corner, after several streets which led us into a much more "up market" area, they'd disappeared. The only possible place they could have gone was into the reception foyer of an impressive apartment block. This entrance was off a smart road and the front of the building was facing the sea.

On entering a dim lobby, which looked dark after leaving bright sunlight, we were beckoned by a dapper little wallah in an exceptionally clean, white galabiyah, with a red fez on his head. No words were exchanged, a finger was placed on his lips to indicate we must be very quiet and he ushered us into a magnificent Edwardian lift with open lattice-work sliding doors.

Still perfectly silent, he stopped and released us into a marbled corridor along which we crept to our respective rooms. The door at the far end was half open and disclosed members of a patently wealthy family taking coffee in small cups. The reason for the high price we'd paid became obvious. Surely the lions' share would end up in the vaults of this family's cash reserves.

The door opened to a large bedroom – and what a room! Big windows gave views out to sea. Massive colonial furniture complemented the huge immaculate bed in their midst. Big mirrors adorned every wall and little Danielle was seated in a plush armchair. Well, if I was indeed about to lose my virginity, it was going to be in some style.

All began to happen in a clinical manner. I was instructed to wash my throbbing manhood and then she fitted a condom, which she supplied, although I'd come with my own Army issue "kit".

I was encouraged to watch her slide off her clothing. She had an adolescent, girl's figure, a lovely warm brown. Definitely not all boobs and bumps. She then assisted me to strip – this on my part, was done in a frenzy of unseemly haste.

Lowering herself back onto the bed she offered herself quickly and willingly to my frantic approach. Having guided me, she closed her eyes and, perhaps prepared herself for some degree of pleasure. Not to be!! The wondrous build up to this moment of satisfaction, had made such demands on my containment, that literally, within seconds it was all over. I think this came as just as big a surprise to her as it did to me. So the next while was spent in some apologetic confusion and in allowing her to savour the answer to her question,

"Ees first time, yes?"

Ismailia bridging the "Sweet Water' Canal

Tank Graveyard El Alamein

She seemed nearly as happy as I was, to discover that was indeed the case.

After a while she washed us both, we dressed, kept our eyes discreetly on the hallway to await the others, and, after some more small-talk we vacated "The Boudoir".

Having regrouped, the four of us exchanged our experiences. Somewhat bawdy, but nevertheless, honest accounts were savoured. Little blonde Evans was his garrulous and excited self but seemed, like me, to have failed to give lasting satisfaction, it being his first coupling too. Bill Edmunds recounted a rather understated satisfaction. Jock Crawford then amazed us by saying that his girl had offered him a free session the next day. This was surely unusual, but easily explained. He'd amused us often enough, demonstrating his attribute by walking naked up and down the middle of our hut, with his tin hat perched on his aroused manhood. The "tin hat", steel really, with heavy lining, was not a lightweight object! N.B. He did go the next day and claim his prize.

After some discussion, it was agreed that we should all repair to the prophylactic centre. This was a small building located right on the waterfront promenade. Staffed by Royal Medical Corps personnel, its function was venereal disease prevention. Names and service numbers were recorded and a slip issued to prove attendance. Each man was given a kit and shown to his own, small cubicle. It contained a powder to prevent a dose of "the crabs", or other similar mites and a small tube of cream with a tapered nozzle. This had to be inserted and squeezed up the penis, all a bit of a laugh. Attendance at this centre was particularly important to married servicemen. Should one catch VD and be hospitalised, his wife's support allowance would be stopped and she may well have been informed of the reason why. Recorded attendance insured against this potentially devastating predicament.

Another day we joined a trip to El Alamein, in company of others from the leave camp. We travelled in an open army truck, along the coast road to this important landmark in the fortunes of the North African desert campaign. It seemed such a small distance from Alex, when viewed with the realization of how near Rommel had come to conquering Egypt. It was a desolate sight: an area covered with the remains of many tanks and vehicles from both armies; just a new plaque identifying it as El Alamein and a few urchins who approached timidly for baksheesh, while their elders kept their distance.

All too soon, the degenerate two weeks ended and we reported back to T.E.K. Many were the heavily embroidered tales related to the crew of Hut 23.

Then came the orders that a number of us were to pack our kit and entrain for a refresher course in bullshit at Ferry Point. This is located at the point where the Suez Canal opens out into Lake Timsah, just north of Ismailia and was, as presumably it still is, where a ferry links the Egyptian west bank with the Sinai east one. The ferry, quite small, was propelled by the chain system, the chain being picked up off the canal bed, passed through a revolving cog wheel and dropped back down.

It was fascinating to watch the proud, nomadic Arabs, heads swathed in chequered cloth, sometimes with their camels and looking like something from the "Laurence of Arabia" film set. These tribesmen from the Sinai Desert submitted reluctantly to search by the Egyptian customs officers, who had a small office building on site.

Our camp was right there. Much blancoing, parading and marching had to be endured. This annoyance was off-set by the close proximity to Ismailia which was

Me with Keith Herbert M.P. Enjoying a bottle of Stella

only a brisk walk away. The return journey, after the customary liquid refreshment, was generally accompanied by off-tune rendering of many songs, for example, "Show me the way to go home", "There's a long, long trail a winding to my dreams", "It's a long way to Tipperary", disturbing the silence of magical, moonlit nights.

Because the camp was on the Suez bank, swimming was a constant relaxation. The canal is not very wide and easy to swim. This exercise resulted in my discovery that I did, after all, possess pectoral muscles!

When approaching the canal from a distance, while a large ship was passing through, it gave the impression that it was

On the Sinai side of suez. Left to right Ivan Turner, Johnny Knolwes, Bob Weeks, Alun Jones, Jocj Curran, Nipper Wiseman and yours truely

sailing across the desert – another interpretation of the phrase, "ships of the desert" more commonly applied to camels.

One ship passed through, crowded with hard, sun-blackened, "old soldiers" returning home after years of conflict in the Far East. Shouted exchanges of conversation were possible and we delighted in telling them,

"Get some service in" and

"Get your knees brown."

The ship was The Monarch of Bermuda.

A keen eye had to be kept on the approach of large vessels. There is a very strict imposition of a speed limit on them, especially as the canal offers a very narrow passage.

One day a group of us had swum to the far bank to laze in the sand and sun when an aircraft carrier was seen about to enter. The passage of such a large vessel should not be a problem! In fact the screws draw water away, causing quite a drop in depth, thereby leaving us well above the water-line. As this happened we were suddenly aware that the deck rails were lined with a galaxy of young, briefly clad, sunburnt, white girls, only yards away. They were cheering and waving very enthusiastically, probably because some of us had shed our trunks to sunbathe and were waving with such gusto, completely forgetting that every body bit was waving in unison.

The carrier made its slow pass and then came an unexpected return wash of the water that reached and washed away our belongings, which had been left well above the normal water line. The carrier was H.M.S. Victorious and was taking six hundred Aussie war brides to Blighty. I expect they had very mixed feelings when they reached that cold and savagely rationed country.

On getting back to T.E.K. I was pleasantly surprised to find my neighbour, Keith Herbert, from Great Barrington, had been posted there. He is a little older than me and had been soldiering in the Far East. Volunteers had been called for to join the Military Police, with the promise that they would leave India. He hardly expected to end up in the Egyptian desert.

After overcoming a natural reluctance to visit a C.M.P. (Corps of Military Police) camp, I found him and we enjoyed swapping experiences, news from home and downing a few bottles of Stella. His duties included raids into the local native villages to attempt to recover some of the W.D. (War Department) property, which was stolen in quite impressive amounts – this, despite the fact that this huge garrison was encircled by barbed wire, extensive minefields and regular patrols. As for patrols, my experience had been mostly limited to reclining on my bed. Much of the patrolling was done by German prisoners of war in the charge of a few squaddies!! Keith told me that such raids were quite dangerous and that some deadly resistance was always possible. The minefield hazard was overcome by the Arabs driving goats ahead.

The whole encampment was totally bereft of any female staff. Then, some optimistic brigadier or general decided to introduce an A.T.S. company, who would help out in offices and canteens. This information was hailed with disbelief and excitement. Their arrival was the cause of many fantasies but reality soon emerged. With such a huge complement of men the girls were able to pick and choose. Officers and N.C.O's were obviously the lucky ones while the rest of us barely glimpsed any of them.

H.M.S. Victorious carrying 600 Aussie brides to blighty

The whole exercise was quickly aborted after only three weeks and they were hurriedly evacuated. It seems that some enterprising beast had slipped some "Spanish Fly" into a drink or sweetmeat. This strangely named concoction is a very strong aphrodisiac and could be purchased in small, yellow wrapped cubes. There ensued what is now known as a "gang bang", even ending, we were told, with the unfortunate girl offering herself to some of the locals. Doubtless there was some exaggeration to this tale, but presumably most was true. A very sordid affair.

CHAPTER SEVEN

Mutiny

At the end of the war all personnel were given demobilization numbers. Those who had been unlucky enough to have served throughout had the lowest numbers. Indeed, some of those who had been members of the Territorial Army pre-war, had been called up months before hostilities began, and served close to seven years. My number was 62 and the "old hands" made fun of me and said that I would be an old man before my release.

Then all of a sudden a crisis caused it all to be suspended for six months. Some of the trouble was caused by a difficulty in integrating so many new civilians in such a short time.

Soon word got around that there was a movement afoot to protest "en masse" against it. All "other ranks" were invited to meet at the camp football ground on the morning of Sunday, November 10th 1946 to organize some sort of action. The football ground had never seen such a crowd. Groups of khaki clad figures homed in from all directions.

It was obvious that a core of leaders had organized themselves and from their vantage point, on tables, they shouted out instructions. The general idea was to refuse to go to the workshops the next day. The movement was carried unanimously and the meeting broke up.

Then to our astonishment we found, on leaving, that the "proper army", the infantry, had appeared. They came with bren-gun carriers and formed a loose circle around us. Others made themselves obvious as they crouched on roofs, rifles and machine guns at the ready. We were marched away, flanked by riflemen and dispersed to our respective camps, being left in no doubt that we would report for duty the next day. Notices were posted which made it plain to us that there is no such thing as a "strike" in the Army and that by "King's Regulations" we were committing mutiny.

Certainly no-one was shot, but next morning each individual was called into an office and grilled. As the first one came out we questioned him on the nature of the interview.

"Tell the bastards nothing you don't have to" was the

4 ACQUITTED AT KASSASSIN

FOUR of the ten NCO's and men who have been on trial at Kassassin Court Martial since January 28, on a joint charge of "conspiring to cause mutiny in H.M. Forces," in November last, were acquitted at yesterday's hearing. The findings in respect of the six other accused will be promulgated later.

The four acquitted men are: Corporal Lamont, Pte. Jones, Pte. O'Neill, and Pte. Carson.

The other accused are: Sgt. R.F. Hughes, Cpl. Walker, Pte. Bradley, Pte. Pountney, Pte. Street, and Pte. Moore.

Never Been Told

Mr. Pritt's associate in the Defence, Mr. John Lattey, called to the witness box the six accused found guilty, who testified that they had never been told what a mutiny was and had no idea that a mutiny was less than an armed rising against officers.

Mr. Lattey then addressed the Court in a mitigation plea, saying that in view of their youth, the three months' detention, and their clean past record, the Court should be as lenient as possible.

None of the accused wished to say anything.

The Court was then concluded. — Reuter.

message.

On entering, I found some unfamiliar officers sitting behind a large desk, while the sergeant who had brought me in stood behind me and ordered me to salute and give my name and army number.

"Did you attend a meeting at the football pitch?"

"Yes sir."

"Did you know it was mutiny and a very serious offence?"

"No sir."

"Do you know the organizers?"

"No sir, too far away."

"Are you reporting back to your workshop?"

"Yes sir."

Another salute, an about turn, a quick exit and it was all over.

Not quite. On returning to the workshop, I, amongst others, decided to test some AEC Matador chassis, drove them to the area where some infantry boys were still standing guard and did some creditable "wheelies". The sand and the dust came up in clouds to the annoyance and discomfort of the stern infantrymen. Eventually ten men were charged with inciting mutiny. They were all placed under close arrest until the trial. I still have the cuttings from "The Egyptian Times" and will try to condense the reports.

The accused spent some three months in a recently vacated P.O.W. (Prisoner of War) camp, No. 305, at Tahag. Then came a court martial at Kassassin.

An eminent Q.C., Mr. Pritt, came from London to defend the prisoners at the hearing, which started on January 28th. He was joined by his associate, Mr. John Lattey.

They heard that a meeting had been held at 117 Shed on November 9th to discuss action because of "the prevalent feeling of dissatisfaction among the garrison over demob and to give that dissatisfaction a definite form".

After two days of prosecution evidence, Mr. Pritt said,

"The eyes of Egypt and of other countries are on this courtroom and it is everybody's duty to carry out the proceedings impartially."

He gave his reasons for not wishing to call the defendants to give evidence.

"It is reasonable to say that these men have been tortured enough by being bullied, cajoled, deceived, lied to and threatened by Major Hynes. Such methods were an eternal disgrace to the British Army. A number of prosecution witnesses were put in filthy detention cells at P.O.W. 305 camp."

Colonel Strong, asked about conditions, could not say they were revolting, but cramped. He said that he did not smell the latrines that German P.O.W's had left behind and as far as he was concerned the only room for improvement was with regard to the lack of space.

Eventually four of the ten N.C.O's and men were acquitted: Corporal Lamont, Privates Jones, O'Neill and Carson. Mr. Lattey then called to the witness box the six accused found guilty: Sergeant Hughes, Corporal Walker and Privates Bradley, Pountney, Street and Moore.

He then addressed the Court in a mitigation plea saying that, in view of their youth, their three months detention and their clean past record, the court should be as lenient as possible.

I never heard much of the eventual fate of these six chaps who had, after all, only called for a peaceful demonstration and, who like me, were totally unaware that in the army's book we were mutineers!

CHAPTER EIGHT

The Joys of Aprés Demob

Then one day I was called into our workshop C.O.'s office. There was a quite relaxed atmosphere as he told me,

"Your army records show that you have a School Certificate. You are to be offered the rank of Staff Sergeant and to be transported to Haifa. Here you will assist in educating soldiers in preparation for their return to 'civvy street'. Are you willing to accept this offer?"

This was a development straight out of the blue. I'm sure I should have taken time to consider it. My response was immediate,

"No thankyou sir, I'd rather stay here."

It was patently obvious in my mind (though not stated), that such a posting could well mean my retention beyond my present demob date.

Also I knew that my father was making representation to our local M.P., Mr. W.S. Morrison, who at that time was Speaker of the House of Commons, for my early demob on what was called "B release". This procedure was set up so that members of the Armed Forces could be allowed out ahead of their normal date, to assist in businesses, where, like my father's, they would be a real asset. Many a time later, I had cause to wonder whether I'd been a fool to reject such an opportunity, but the call to get home was too strong and I probably did the right thing.

As spring dragged on into summer, and believe me, the Egyptian summer out in the desert gets really hot, I was allocated five weeks leave, 17th May to 22nd June, in the U.K. The old boys came home on a scheme called P.Y.T.H.O.N, which gave them a much longer leave. Others, like me, were awarded L.I.A.P, which was leave in lieu of P.Y.T.H.O.N.

Much preparation was required, not least to cajole the Egyptian upholsterer in our workshops to make a large kit-bag. It was something like double the size of the regulation one. Made in stout, white calico with all the brass eyelets, it was a masterpiece of construction. I still have it bearing the written messages of goodwill and signatures of several of my army friends. This essential bit of kit was to allow for the sealed tins of 50 cigarettes, which cost two shillings, (ten pence in current money!), that I would take with me. Players, Gold Flake and export Woodbines. The Woodbines were the same size as the others and were perhaps, the best of all. Some twenty tins were accommodated, packed in the central section with the normal kit above and below.

I was the only one on my draft from Hut 27, but would be joined at Port Said by a shipload from all points of the Middle East.

After a decent "piss up" at the N.A.A.F.I. the night before leaving, I watched the others go off to their workshops and was picked up and transported to Tel el Kebir railway station. At Port Said we were crushed on to a tank landing craft and crossed the Suez to a transit camp. This was surrounded by a ten foot wire fence and was tented. We had to wait for the ship to come in and spent some time watching from behind the fence.

When it did arrive it was one of those "famous" American built Liberty ships. They were produced on a massive production line system and were welded together instead of the traditional riveted construction. They had something of a reputation for breaking in half in stormy seas. When we left to board, it was patently obvious who were the officers. Their many bags and boxes were carried by German P.O.W's; we struggled under our own kit.

The ship was the "H.T. Stamford Victory". As soon as we had been allocated our few feet of space and discovered that we were to sleep in hammocks, lashed to any available stanchion, we all crowded on deck to watch our departure. The usual optimistic gaggle of "bum boats" were plying their trade – squaddies haggling away and buying various, doubtful bargains.

The clatter of the huge anchor chain being recovered announced our imminent departure and we slid quietly away. In this present-day world of cruising, it may seem a waste of time to elaborate on it.

First, we passed close to the French battleship "Duquesne", fully dressed with all flags flying, then the big, colonial style offices of the Canal Company and after another sighting of the ill-fated De Lesseps statue, we entered the Mediterranean.

We were cosseted, fed and watered like returning heroes, as indeed some of the complement may well have been. After the early "boat drill", still deemed to be important, mines still being a problem, we could settle down and enjoy our cruise.

The Stamford Victory was not built for speed and we had days of blissful idling before passing through the Straits of Gibraltar. The Rock was bathed in sunlight and a number of grey warships could be seen at anchor. The Bay of Biscay lived up to its reputation and the ship bucked and wallowed its way through. What with all this movement and the thought that the ship might break in two, many were feeling apprehensive. Typically, under these conditions, a large percentage of the lads went green and spent much time below deck near to the "heads". The decks became dangerous where some of them didn't make it and were sea-sick all over the place. I've always been lucky and never been so afflicted.

We were informed that we were to dock at Liverpool. As the sea finished turning from a deep blue to a cold grey we watched a coastline emerge. This was North Wales and soon a boat came to meet us. It was the Port of Liverpool pilot boat and as we lost way and stopped it despatched a small craft to convey their pilot aboard. On completing a seemingly hazardous exercise, where the poor chap had to shin up a rope ladder, we headed for the Mersey. Here, soon after passing the

Crossing Suez to H.T. Stamford Victory our transport home

Awaiting Liberty ship- was there ever a bigger kit-bag than mine?

Liver Building with its two exotic Liver birds and having seen the "Ferry over the Mersey", we docked.

Disembarkation completed, we were lined up near His Majesty's Custom Shed. Customs officers came out and worked their way down the lines where we stood with our kit and kitbags. I had some misgivings about the size of my kitbag when contrasted with those around me. When the officer stood in front of me he proceeded to read out a list of all items considered to be contraband and those acceptable.

Typical chatty postcard from my mother

"Have you anything to declare?"

"No" and off he went to the next man.

I believe it to have been a formality. No-one was searched as far as I could see and the most inefficient of them could have detected my unease and jumbo kitbag.

We were soon taken to the railway station, given all necessary documents and sent off to our separate home addresses.

Obviously the general public in my carriage knew nothing about the easy army life I'd been leading and went out of their way to offer cigarettes, and, having noticed my heavy suntan, something not usual in those bleak days, tried to be helpful in every way. It was an astonishing ego trip, even though undeserved.

My "Combined Pass and Railway Ticket" took me to Oxford Station. Looking at the document, I see that it still contains the unused section for my return to Maghull – more about that later!

With my excitement mounting, the train slowed and pulled up to the loud accompaniment of a local voice announcing, "Oxford, Oxford", and I hastily de-trained. A phone call, answered by my happy and relieved mother, produced a quick promise that my father would pick me up just as soon as he could get there. In no time at all I saw the faithful Austin 10 speed to the station foyer. My father, never given to demonstrate his feelings, actually grinned and treated me even more like the adult that I had become in those few short years. I wouldn't be twenty one until next month. It was a wonderful time, both on the journey home and at home, catching up with all the news and gossip and me trying to get back to normality. My mother had written copiously and regularly, and I still treasure the many letters and local scene postcards she sent me. They reopen many memories of our somewhat isolated village and village people of sixty years ago.

My consuming priority was to get my little Morris back on the road. I'd taken the precaution of blocking her up, wheels free, in the big barn and there she was, ready to get going. Next day I was away to Gloucester to get my driving licence and so, with the insurance cover note written out by my father, who was an agent, I was immediately mobile.

While abroad, many happy hours were spent writing letters. I had kept up a regular correspondence with three girls – the two Jeans at Filkins as well as Mimi at Bicester. They all had to be visited. This enviable situation was also augmented by another commitment.

Jack Stocks was home from the Navy, having survived convoy work, doing several of the crucial trips to Archangel, taking equipment and stores to the beleaguered Russians; Maurice Herbert from the Tank Corps, safely through the Italian campaign and his brother Phillip from the R.A.F.

I was soon informed about the departure of the Land Girls. The previous winter, 46/47 had been

My Morris with a bevy of Land Girls

particularly severe. My mother had written week after week, with photographs, about the exceptional snowfalls. The villages had been cut off and it was many days before the Barrington to Rissington road was opened. Most of the work was done by men with shovels.

The hostel, Sir Stafford Cripps' house, was no more. Generous fires in the huge drawing-room fireplace had been kept going at full blast. Unfortunately, unknown to the Warden or the girls, an exposed beam in the chimney ignited, and set off a major conflagration in the middle of the night. The girls were asleep in bed when the house filled with smoke, followed by the heat of the flames. Some of the bedrooms on the third floor had dormer windows in the roof. The three girls in those bedrooms were Mavis Wilkinson, Elsie Worral and Mary White.

In terror they all huddled together in one of the windows. The roofs, like the ground, were covered in snow and ice. Elsie lost her grip and slipped down the roof to the ground below. She sustained a fractured pelvis, which was the most serious injury in the hostel. It could have been fatal because she lost consciousness and was found with her head and upper body resting on the, thankfully, frozen ice of the water-filled moat. Several local fire brigades came to the rescue. The girls, still clad in their night-clothes, were taken home, calmed and pampered by a number of understanding villagers. All their belongings and clothing were lost. When they were ready, they were transferred to a hostel at Starveall Farm, just north of Woodstock.

Starveall had been another R.A.F. satellite Landing Ground and had closed in September 1945, after having been home to many stored aircraft, mainly Spitfires. As was common at that time, many useful hutments were left vacant and were utilised by the W.L.A. (Womens' Land Army).

I then found myself divided between going to see my "steady" girlfriend, Mimi, at Bicester, or becoming part of the lecherous gang chasing up to Woodstock at every opportunity. There were still very few cars around and to own one was again, a huge bonus.

Land Girls, mostly "Townies," were thought by the locals to be "fast and loose" and were given a bad reputation. Believe me, they did not deserve it, but many were fun-loving extroverts and very good company, whilst retaining their honour.

Yes, many could drink the local lads under the table. Those that insisted on drinking very expensive Pimms No. 1, soon found themselves avoided, on a principle of unsustainable cost! Pubs and weekend dances or "hops", were about their only possible recreation, giving them a chance to meet the local lads, who flocked round them like bees to a honey pot.

I escorted several young ladies round the many Woodstock and district pubs and exciting times they were. Memories blurred in an alcoholic haze.

Questions run through my mind.

Why did a girl being driven back to camp by Philip Herbert, pick a quarrel with her Land Army

Path to Post Office during the winter of 46/47

friend and decide to pick up the car jack which was lying on the floor and hurl it through the car's plate glass door window?

Why, when driving Jack Stocks home after a last drink or two in The Bell at Long Hanborough, did he suddenly produce the massive key out of the pub's front door?

Expressing some concern about the point of this, I asked what he was going to do with it.

"I don't know", he said as he opened the window and threw it into the roadside hedge.

Many people might ask why, when Mervyn and I drove up to the front of the hostel the doors and the windows were jammed with girls chanting to me,

"Take him away, we don't want him here."

Why they should have been driven to such a united protest can only say much for his ability to love them and leave them! But not this time, when they were all mates.

Then one evening in The Crown at Woodstock, I was introduced to this lovely, bubbly, little girl, Mavis Wilkinson and a lasting attachment was formed.

I now had two lovely girlfriends. My visits to Bicester became less frequent and the whole situation became a balancing act. I am ashamed to say that I allowed the "logistics" to rule my heart, Bicester was so much further than Woodstock and the lure of wild parties with my friends and our girls nearer home, tipped the balance. After watching this "menage à trois" go on for a long time, my mother confronted me with reality and told me, quite plainly, that it shouldn't continue. She knew how long I had known Mimi and just how let down she must feel – I've felt a rotter ever since.

Mavis, Elsie and Betty. Back row 3rd, 4th and 5th from left

Datkota at Broadwell, Mavis's boyfriend centre, arrowed

After some couple of weeks of my leave, I was contacted to inform me that my "B release" had come through and I was to take a further three weeks demob leave.

During this time, Mavis and other friends were posted to another hostel. This was a large house, "Goldmore", which fronted on to Peppard Common near Nettlebed. Her friend Elsie, who had joined the Land Army the same day and lived in Wednesbury, very near to Mavis' home in Walsall, was transferred with her.

In high summer the surrounding area was a delight to discover. Driving through the quiet lanes, bereft of traffic, Rotherfield Greys, Goring, Streetley, even Henley-on-Thames and other such jewels, were all there to enjoy. Lazy days by the river, all with convenient hostelries to savour. The roads between Nettlebed and Peppard were still lined with caches of bombs – as were many between Little Rissington and Bledington – under covers shaped like miniature Nissan huts.

To make all things perfect for the winding up of my military service, I was ordered to report to my old R.E.M.E. unit at Bicester. The same regimental sergeant-major was still there in the regimental office. Not the cold, hard man I had known before, but changed into a human who could have been celebrating the return of a prodigal son. This attitude met me all over the camp. Unbelievable! I was instructed to go the next day, in my own car, to a demob centre, Jack Stocks came with me. The drill was to go in one end of the building, select a suit, a hat and other items and leave the exit with a large cardboard box containing them.

I'd never had to buy any clothing on my own before, so in my rush to get away, I spent scant time over the selection process. There were long racks of suits of varied colours and sizes and on finding one that fitted, I also picked up a trilby hat – these trilbies being the fashion – and soon was away. I later found that it could have paid dividends to have been more diligent. All manufacturers were called on to supply a percentage of their products to these centres. With care, it was possible to find famous names from Savile Row and the like, to take home.

It was my twenty-first birthday, and after stowing my trophies, we set off on a diversion to Peppard. The girls were already at "home". Mavis had been given the job of caring for the large garden – she became an enthusiastic flower gardener for life and Elsie was helping out on the milk round. A typical, fun-packed evening ensued, drinking plenty and smoking our heads off with yet another of my duty-free tins of fags. As always, I left the remaining cigarettes for the girls. My stock was getting depleted by now.

The drive home was nearly marred by accident. The road through Nuneham Courtney is flanked by mature trees and, fuelled by drink and a taxing day, I nodded off and nearly wrapped us around one of them. This near incident prompted Jack to tell me to,

"Put the windscreen down."

The little car was equipped with a

Jack Stocks, mervyn Garratt and my Morris 8

screen which would fold forward. The hood being already stowed away, the ensuing gale was a great aid to keeping awake. This was, too often, very necessary. Some catastrophe to have happened on my twenty-first and demob day!

This carefree existence was too good to last. Father reverted to his old, demanding and domineering style and I was soon back in the old routine; working seven days a week at full stretch and finding myself with a mere five pounds a week pay.

Soon after I was back, I noticed that the only lockup garage stayed locked. On asking why, I was told,

"Don't you worry about that."

Curiosity was rewarded when I discovered a pristine Jeep, with all American forces markings, sitting in there. This seemed a bit strange as the only service vehicles beginning to be auctioned off now were British army ones.

Father then told me its pedigree. After D-day, some American soldiers had come back into the area and had become friends with him. One day, one of them said, seemingly in jest,

"How'd you like a Jeep Tom?"

He replied, with a smile,

"That would be great wouldn't it?"

Soon after they were back.

"We've brought your Jeep, Tom."

Tom being totally unprepared and not wishing to lose face said,

"How much do you want for it?"

"Fifty pounds."

He paid up but was at a loss to know what to do with it, and, so there it stood, with no documentation whatsoever and covered in Yankee markings.

Then an army disposal sale was announced at Cornbury Park, Charlbury. There had been previous ones at Toddington and Ashchurch. Father had teamed up with Mr. R.N. Wilmer of Friars Court, Clanfield and they had bought several Jeeps between them. The task of getting them home devolved on Tom. They had to enter the depot, locate and remove the vehicle, and present the bill of sale to the civilian guards at the gates. These fellows took advantage of their situation. Their pals inside removed distributors, carburettors, rotor arms and petrol pumps, rendering the vehicles useless. The guards then sold them to the new owners, who were only too happy to acquire them. Many were the adventures involved in getting them home. Stanway Hill, still a considerable climb, was a notorious problem to the under-powered towing cars of those days.

Cornbury Park was a huge sale. Row after row of Jeeps, Dodges, Bedfords and so on. It went on for days and father, again with Mr. Wilmer, spent a lot of time there. He'd ring up and tell me to come over and tow these Jeeps that he had bought out of the Park.

By this time we had thrown caution to the

Elsie and Mavis

winds and were using the American Jeep as the tow vehicle. The lack of a licence presented no problem, as we could use trade plates, which can be affixed to any vehicle in the charge of a garage owner. How others who had "acquired" questionable ownership fared, I don't know. Rumour had it that farmer Frank Walker of Kencot built his into the middle of a haystack.

My first job at the auction was to remove the vehicles to a small paddock just outside the Park. This I could accomplish with what is called an A frame, shackled either side of the front bumper and attached to the pintle of the towing Jeep. This arrangement is such a surprise when it is first used; the towed vehicle is driverless and follows exactly, the steering wheel moving round and back with no hands required. So after moving and parking several, I would tow the last one home. Then after some sustenance I would pick up Jack and Mervyn. Our first move was to tow a Jeep through the very quiet streets of Charlbury and unhitch on the bank by Wychwood Forest, return for a second one on the A frame and now, out of sight of Charlbury police, rope the parked one behind and drive off with two on tow and Mervyn driving the third one. We then delivered them to Clanfield, Jack bringing Mr. Wilmer's Jeep back to repeat the operation. Back to Charlbury and fetch the last ones back to the garage.

Both farmyard barns at Clanfield and the garage space were soon filled with all these vehicles. Altogether, from several auctions, some one hundred and forty Jeeps were purchased. The average price was eighty pounds and, after refurbishment, they were sold for one hundred and twenty – a good profit in those days, particularly as we three chaps were never paid for our labours! Mr. Wilmer's Jeep seemed to run on the usual mixture of petrol and T.V.O. He was a strict Chapel man, and one petrol delivery driver, when at the garage, told us that he'd turned up to deliver fuel on a Sunday and been sent away. Another, wishing to have a smoke round the corner, away from his tanker, was upbraided by Mr. Wilmer, who told him to put it out and, that if God had wanted us to smoke, he would have put a little chimney on our heads.

Most of these Jeeps finished up on local farms. My army experience with them was invaluable and we had the maintenance of them for years to come. Our furthest sale was to the Banwell Castle Estate in Somerset. Both Jack and Mavis came with a second vehicle and after the delivery we were able to divert to Cheddar Gorge and Goughs Caves.

Many years later I rescued the worn out remains of three farmers Jeeps. From these I was able to rebuild one complete and near perfect example. Sadly lack of garage space has caused me to pass it on to another good home. YFF 344 with whose existence I had been so closely related for fifty years is now preserved for posterity.

Then Mavis and Elsie got themselves transferred to a hostel near Shilton. It was part of the Broadwell Airfield complex. The R.A.F. had left and a group of huts was allocated to the Land Army. This was only a few minutes away from home. Elsie was now with Mervyn and we made a good foursome. The area contained the camp morgue, complete with marble slab, and though I revolted at the idea, tales circulated of couples who had used the slab as a love nest!

During my time abroad and while Mavis was at Filkins, before the fire, she had a liaison with one of the Dakota air crew that had been flying from here. The air crews got very friendly with the Land Girls and would fly low over them, waving to them at work in the fields. The girls were in great demand and were

Recreation Room, Broadwell W.L.A.

Airspeed Horsa Glider

Dakota towing Horsa glider. Both showing D. Day identification white stripes

organized into parties and transported to different venues for Saturday night dances. Also, while there, she was sent to work for Bob Stokes, the local dairy man.

She could always raise a laugh about delivering milk in Carterton. She'd just got back to the milk float when a man asked her,

"Can you sell me a bottle of milk please?"

"Of course."

Sale made, Bob came back,

"What did that chap want?"

"A bottle of milk."

"Where did you get it from?"

"One of those."

"That's all right then", with a look of relief. Bob had recognised a Milk Board Inspector. She then found out that Bob had watered some of the milk and she might well have sold him a wrong one.

Meanwhile, two other girls, Anne Bradley and Betty Colloby, were being romanced by the brothers, Philip and Maurice Herbert – aforementioned Barrington lads. For whatever reason the girls decided to move away and transferred to the Cornish W.L.A. Not to be outdone their beaux undertook the long trek to the Penzance area on several occasions. Philip had this old Rover. It used nearly as much oil as petrol and left a dense cloud of smoke behind it. It was so bad that one day, from a vantage point on the A40, I could see at least a mile ahead and correctly identified the plume of smoke in the distance as the Rover. It was, and as it passed, the bell like sound, which a large detached shock absorber made as it constantly banged against the chassis, confirmed it. Cornwall was a long way and included an overnight stop on Bodmin Moor. The girls were persuaded to return and both couples got married.

Mavis then transferred to Cokethorpe House near Witney. The Land Army had taken over part of the mansion, while the family still occupied the rest; it is now a private school. I'd sometimes pick her up in a Jeep and one day, on the A40, the petrol pump packed up. Not to be outdone, I fixed a gravity feed. This required Mavis to sit on the front wing, holding a spare can of petrol lodged on the bonnet, from which a plastic tube ran down to the carburettor!

While Mavis was at Cokethorpe we got engaged to marry. I couldn't take time off during the day and so gave her money to buy the ring of her choice! I have since realised what an unconventional family mine was and just what she was letting herself in for.

I was dominated by a father with whom I was unable to confide or discuss my private life and who had already declined to have anything to do with my sister Doreen's wedding – I had to give her away at church! He did not wish to meet her husband and in fact did not see his granddaughter until she was two years old, even though they were only at Wheatley, where her husband had a garage with petrol pumps. He was completely disinterested in my girlfriends, who, like, Doreen's husband, were never, ever invited home. My mother, who was such a tender, loving and sociable person, must have felt terribly lonely and frustrated.

Mavis, who had never been confirmed in church, took confirmation instruction in the small, private chapel in Cokethorpe grounds, followed by a very impressive confirmation service in Christ Church Cathedral, Oxford. This service, which I attended, was taken by the Bishop of Dorchester.

Then, in July 1948, Mavis resigned from the Land Army and went home to Walsall. There, being already in possession of a life-saver's certificate, she found a job as a pool attendant at the open-air swimming pool in Walsall Arboretum. I visited regularly, this being years before any thought of motorways and spaghetti junction. The A34 went straight through Brum. The first time I went, I reached the centre, and to find which road to take, I pulled in to the curb outside John Lewis in New Street, got out of my car as there was very little traffic, (imagine doing it now!), and asked directions from the first man that I saw. He pointed to a set of tram-lines (trams were still running) and in a very Brummie accent said,

"Yo see them tram-lines, yo follow them and yo'm get to Walsall."

I was in another world, and when reaching Walsall, it was all leather workers and miners. I felt, and I was, in my country clothes, a hick from the sticks. South Street, my goal, was a typical inner city street, with the pub, The Lamb, at its centre. Mine was the only car parked in it. It was savagely parochial – all friends and "enemies", but very happy to welcome Mavis Wilkinson's boyfriend. Huge trays of mild beer slopped their way to the company in the pub, which was virtually, their only place of relaxation; the premises were again, typical. The entrance passage leading direct to the off-licence shutter, the right hand room full of hard drinking men, many still in their working clothes, even on a Sunday. The room to the left, more of a "snug", filled up with men and their demure wives, dressed in their best clothes.

Never having encountered the Salvation Army before, it was an education to see them each Sunday morning, come into the pub and be treated with the same dignity, as that which they themselves radiated, as they collected pennies from willing hands. The sight of them reforming into their band and marching off down the street, the drums and tambourines, keeping time with their brass instruments, was very uplifting.

Back home, more activity by the M.O.D. was seen. Most of the surviving Wellington bombers were flown into Rissington for disposal. They were taken down a service road to a field some half a mile south of the airfield and scrapped. Each made only a few pounds, mainly for the aluminium content. There was a lot of burning of the doped fabrics.

My Morris car now boasted a set of easy clean wheels. The originals had been wire-spoked, but these were pressed steel with virtually new, "balloon" 16 inch tyres, instead of the narrow "17" ones. They had been supplied by some British Army lads who were involved with the disposal of army vehicles and been "nicked" off some two-wheel trailers with the same wheel stud fittings – a cheap and great improvement!

During the latter part and for quite some time after the war, local farmers were able to stay productive with the help of prisoners of war. They included Chris Eden, a German; a Yugoslav, Johnny Puschnic and an Italian. Johnny stayed and worked for farmer Fred Arkell until his retirement. After the war he was able to send for his wife and three children to join him. Ivan, Joe and sister Sophie, who later died in an horrific car accident, were soon presented with a baby brother, Philip.

Meanwhile, I received a letter, signed by M. Wingfield and B.Arthurs, from the **Welcome Home Fund**.

This stated:

> We, the undersigned, have been entrusted with the disposal of the above fund, which was organized by a local committee. A total of £236/5s/0d is available for distribution among the men and women who served during the War from Great and Little Barrington.
>
> We have pleasure in asking you to accept the enclosed £5.5s.0d (five guineas) in appreciation of your services in the forces, and we welcome you home to your villages.
>
> The committee hopes that perhaps you will be able to purchase something to remind you of your service and safe return.

Mavis soon tired of Walsall and took a job as nanny with Guy Woodin's family at Staytes Farm, Swinbrook. She lived in and looked after the son and daughter.

CHAPTER NINE

The Home Straight

A long time passed, too long I suppose, before both Mavis and I, and Mervyn and Elsie got around to setting a wedding date in September 1951. As we each wished to attend the others matrimonials, we decided the dates should be two weeks apart. After tossing a coin, Mervyn was the first, on the 8th September and ours was September 22nd.

We had a wonderful wedding in Caldmore Green parish church in Walsall and a proper feast afterwards. Many Gloucestershire people attended and Jack Stocks was my best man. I hardly need to say that my father did not attend. He had kept me working to the last moment, I even had to get a hair cut and buy new shoes in Walsall that morning! Alan White, a taxi proprietor from Taynton brought my mother, sister and family friends, refusing payment! No father again!

After a honeymoon in Llandudno – where we were late arriving at the hotel having taken the wrong road at Betws-y-coed and going all the way through Bethesda, before taking the coast road back – we came back to 13 Great Barrington. This house, despite its unlucky number, was chosen out of four possibilities that the Wingfield estate offered. The rent was ten shillings a week and I still have the first receipt for it. Because of the extraordinary situation whereby Mavis had never visited the village, my mother and I had to choose the furnishings and Mavis had never seen any of it. It was one house of very few that had cold water on tap. Nearly everyone had to go to one of three village pumps. It was many years later that I appreciated just what a shock it must have been for my new wife to be without a bathroom or inside toilet. There was only a vaulted "privy" outside the back door. This, on inspection, was found to be infested with all kinds of beetles and such like, when viewed through the hole in the wooden seat. My answer to that problem was to sprinkle a liberal amount of paraffin into the recess and set the thing alight. After a minor explosion and a reasonable conflagration, it was deemed acceptable for use.

We lived there for several years, but Mavis, who loved kids, failed to have any of her own. Tests were performed on us both, all of which found no particular reason for this. I'm sure that modern gynaecological practices could have solved our predicament.

By now Mavis was getting distressed and depressed and wished for a complete change. My father had held the tenancy for The Barrington New Inn since 1935. He had never run it, but wishing to establish his garage in the outside premises, he sublet the Inn to the existing landlord at the time. This man, Mr. W. Whitlock, had gone bankrupt but was able to start again. The annual rent for the whole premises was £26/0s/0d or 50 new pence per week.

Mavis and I then embarked on a new

My Morris 8 and one of the many jeeps.
The orginal garage forecourt

venture establishing ourselves as hosts when Mr. Whitlock agreed to vacate and move to The Royal Oak in Burford. We invited Mervyn and Elsie to join us and share the work and the profits. Mervyn and I continued in our respective jobs, taking over the running of the bar at weekends and evenings. With even the best of friends there can be problems when working so closely, and when Elsie became pregnant it was decided that she and Mervyn would move out.

The apprentice Landlord

This left Mavis the superhuman task of running the establishment, the bar, the bed and breakfast accommodation and all my day to day needs as a husband, clean clothes, meals and so on. It was quite obvious that something had to give and she suffered a nervous breakdown, which continued to blight her life at many times over the rest of her life and all because we never had children!

We moved into three upstairs rooms which served as a self-contained flat and found a couple, John and Vera Hauter, who moved in and ran it as their business. This was not really a satisfactory arrangement and it fell apart when Mavis decided that she'd had enough and went back home to Walsall. I found the first week on my own quite bearable, but by the end of the second I was getting desperate. I was able to convince Mavis, by promising to buy a local house, to return. Her decision to come back was also prompted by the reception that she'd received from her mother. That good lady, whose Victorian attitudes had also been passed onto her daughter, told her to come back saying,

"You made your bed and you should lie on it."

After buying one of a small row of cottages in Windrush for the sum of £360/0s.0d, we moved down there. Mavis went to work at an office at Rissington aerodrome. Then my mother died overnight from a massive brain haemorrhage.

My father, after a period of living alone, during which time, hurting from the knowledge that he had lost so much more than he had ever appreciated, moved to live with a woman in Waterperry whom he later married. He did this in haste and lived to regret it. This meant a daily commute and he'd sometimes fail to turn up at the garage, leaving me to cope somehow. After one extended absence, Mavis got very concerned for me and when he eventually turned up, went out and really let fly at him. It was not only a confrontation but, incredibly, after all these years, the first time they had even spoken to each other. No family member had ever taken such a liberty and it was an education to watch him just sit there and take it. It should have been done years before!

He then decided to relinquish the tenancy and the owners, the Wingfield family of Barrington Park, decided to sell it. I tendered a bid of £17,000, which was not accepted, so it went to auction and realized £18,000. Shell petrol company bought it and I became their tenant for the garage business, while they put Jack and Nancy Stocks as caretaker tenants for The Inn.

After five years, during which time I negotiated for a plot of land in the adjoining field, to build a new garage and petrol pump amenities. Shell sold the pub and the new owners changed the name to The Inn for All Seasons.

I moved into the new garage premises in 1964 at exactly the same time as moving in to my present address at Little Barrington, where I'd converted two cottages into one house. They had cost me £2,600/0s/0d and a conversion cost of about £7,000/0s/0d, some difference from its present estimated value of well over half a million. People say that the difference in value is all

Barrington New Inn and garage

relative and geared to inflation. Utter nonsense! I pride myself that I have never needed to borrow any money in my life, but patently I could never afford to buy into one of these villages today. That privilege is now assumed by the "chattering classes" down from the big city with their formidable incomes and fortunes. My house will inevitably share the same fate. I would be sorry to witness it and hope to see my days out in it. Tragically there are only three villagers left here, Charles Sollis, who is over ninety years old, and his wife, Mary, and I, both in our eightieth year. The only continuity with the past will be the Wingfield and Mills families, the hereditary owners of their respective Great and Little Barrington Estates.

Sadly, Mavis died 3rd January 2005, aged eighty years, after many years of gradual progression of debilitating arthritis. Could I be alone in recognising, too late, many of the attributes of a lost spouse?

Front entrance to Inn